PRAISE FOR THE RISE OF SUSTAINABLE GIVING

"In this timely book, Dave Raley offers nonprofit leaders a clear, actionable guide to navigating the new world of subscription giving. His insights will empower organizations to rethink their approach to sustainable fundraising in a practical and inspiring way."

—**Nathan Chappell**,
Coauthor of *The Generosity Crisis*

"Dave's passion for and interest in subscription giving and its ability to help transform organizations and our world shines through. From the stories, examples, and research, everyone will be able to find something that can help them chart a better path to sustainable growth."

—**Brady Josephson**,
VP of Marketing & Growth, charity: water

"Dave Raley's *The Rise of Sustainable Giving* is *the* industry playbook to help nonprofits accelerate sustained, profitable growth. His practical insights, accessible recommendations, and data-informed strategies are highly actionable. This book is a must-read for any leader seeking to build or grow a recurring revenue model in their organization."

—Andrew Olsen,
CFRE, Executive Vice President, Fundraising Solutions, DickersonBakker

"Dave's book offers a great take on the importance and ease of generating subscription donors, a.k.a. sustainers, aka recurring donors. Dave maps out why the growth of subscriptions has had such a positive impact on the rise of subscription giving. He describes how nonprofits and donors alike can benefit from this new 'old' way of giving, how to create critical value propositions, and the best channels and tools to grow."

—Erica Waasdorp,
Monthly Donor Growth and Retention Consultant, A Direct Solution, Author of *Monthly Giving: The Sleeping Giant* and *Monthly Giving Made Easy*

"A complete game changer—*The Rise of Sustainable Giving* is *the* field manual for transforming your entire fundraising program. Read it. Do it."

—Tim Kachuriak,
Founder and Chief Innovation & Optimization Officer, NextAfter

"Dave Raley is one of my most trusted sources for knowing the pulse of the nonprofit sector. In *The Rise of Sustainable Giving*, he shares a compelling case—backed by research—for why recurring giving matters now more than ever. But the real promise here is what can be unlocked for our organizations by shifting our mindsets and actions around this work, and it's all within this book. It's a path to more connection, more engagement, and more sustainability."

—Jon McCoy,
Cofounder and CEO, We Are For Good

"If there was any doubt about the impact of the subscription economy on the rise of recurring giving, this book is your proof. Dave's thoughtful research and personal experiences underscore the importance for nonprofit leaders to strategically plan for the future."

—Dana Snyder,
Author of *The Monthly Giving Mastermind* and
Founder & CEO of Positive Equation

"For nonprofit leaders experiencing the inevitable stress of unpredictable fundraising models, *The Rise of Sustainable Giving* is for you. Dave's data-backed recommendations and forward-thinking perspective offer a clear vision for how nonprofits can navigate the changing landscape of philanthropy."

—Gabe Cooper,
CEO of Virtuous and Author of
The Responsive Nonprofit

"In *The Rise of Sustainable Giving*, Dave Raley offers a fresh take on how nonprofits can leverage the subscription economy to drive lasting impact. His actionable insights provide a clear roadmap for organizations looking to evolve their fundraising strategies."

—Russell James,
JD, PhD, Author of *The Storytelling Fundraiser*
and Professor of Charitable Financial Planning,
Texas Tech University

"With consumers increasingly favoring the subscription economy—where companies are growing over three times faster than traditional models—nonprofits have a tremendous opportunity to capitalize on this trend. In *The Rise of Sustainable Giving*, Dave Raley demonstrates how recurring giving can be a game-changer for organizations, offering practical advice on adapting and thriving. Now is the time for nonprofit leaders to follow Raley's advice and invest in this shift, making it simpler and more seamless for donors to contribute and to achieve sustainable growth while smoothing out the unpredictability of 'lumpy' seasonal giving."

—Donna Tschiffely,
Executive Director, DMAW

"As World Vision's former head of marketing, I thought I knew everything there was to know about recurring giving. Dave has shown me in this book that there's a lot I didn't know. Recurring giving is a must for every organization. Dave shows you why and how."

—Steve Woodworth,
CEO of Masterworks and Former VP of
Marketing World Vision

"Dave Raley's new book, *The Rise of Sustainable Giving,* combines his innovative perspective on today's automatic behavior, emerging trends, and extensive fundraising experiences. He brilliantly makes the case and points the way for nonprofits to seize the current reality. It's time to read this book and put it into practice for your greater good. Don't let this new era of generosity pass you by!"

—Tami Heim,
President & CEO of Christian
Leadership Alliance

"Raley's insightful book delves into the convergence of the subscription model and nonprofit fundraising strategies. *The Rise of Sustainable Giving* serves as a valuable roadmap for leaders aiming to chart a course for their organization's future sustainability."

—Shannon McCracken,
CEO, The Nonprofit Alliance

"Every nonprofit should have a killer sustainer program in the market that their audience loves. Yet, look around, and you'll see how jarringly rare that actually is. Raley's well-researched and clearly written *The Rise of Sustainable Giving* is a timely resource for nonprofit leaders to align their thinking with market realities and pursue the sustainer-forward strategies needed to grow."

—Allen Thornburgh,
Principal & Executive Producer, Sublimity

"In *The Rise of Sustainable Giving*, Dave Raley zeroes in on the factors most imperiling to nonprofit mission advancement, if not their very survivability, and lays out a practical path to a more promising future. Raley shows how an age-old practice can be adapted to current and emerging philanthropic realities but not as a simplistic, single-dimension solution. He brings intelligence, experience, wisdom, and compassion to bear on this topic and a time when all are terribly needed. He writes with crisp, compelling clarity and provides the reader with eminently useful information."

—Jim Langley,
President, Langley Innovations

"Subscription giving is one of the most important opportunities for nonprofits to generate ongoing revenue. Dave Raley offers insightful and practical approaches that nonprofit leaders need to increase their impact on the world."

—Tom Harrison,
CEO Russ Reid Company, Retired

"*The Rise of Sustainable Giving* is packed with actionable insights and real substance. Raley not only dives deep into the heart of the subscription economy but expertly navigates the key strategies for success. This book goes beyond being just a guide—it's a blueprint for innovation."

—Jade Nguyen Swanson,
Former President DMAW and Director of Client Services MESG Marketing

The Rise of Sustainable Giving

The Rise of Sustainable Giving

How the Subscription Economy Is Transforming Recurring Giving and What Nonprofits Can Do to Benefit

Dave Raley

Copyright © 2025 by Dave Raley

All rights reserved. No part of this book may be reproduced, distributed, or transmitted in any form or by any means, including photocopying, recording, or other electronic or mechanical methods, without the written permission from the publisher or author, except as permitted by US copyright law or in the case of brief quotations embodied in a book review.

Disclaimer: Although the publisher and the author have made every effort to ensure that the information in this book was correct at press time and while this publication is designed to provide accurate information in regard to the subject matter covered, the publisher and the author assume no responsibility for errors, inaccuracies, omissions, or any other inconsistencies herein and hereby disclaim any liability to any party for any loss, damage, or disruption caused by errors or omissions, whether such errors or omissions result from negligence, accident, or any other cause.

Cover Design by Nathaniel Roy
Interior Layout and Design by Alice Briggs

ISBNs:
Ebook: 979-8-89165-209-5
Paperback: 979-8-89165-210-1
Hardcover: 979-8-89165-211-8

Published by:
Imago Productions
Poulsbo, WA

In association with
Streamline Books
Kansas City, MO
www.streamlinebookspublishing.com

Dedication

To all leaders passionate about inspiring generosity and the future of philanthropy.

Leadership is influence. If you inspire action—to give, to speak up, to go—you are a leader.

SUSTAINABLE GIVING ASSESSMENT

After years of research and hundreds of hours, we've developed a sustainable giving growth self-assessment for nonprofit leaders and fundraisers.

This free assessment includes twenty questions and takes just ten minutes to complete.

After completing the assessment, you'll receive a personalized report on the next steps you should take to grow your recurring giving program.

You can take the assessment at www.imago.consulting/assessment.

Your personalized results will be a helpful guide as you seek to grow recurring subscription giving.

Take the Sustainable Giving Assessment at
www.imago.consulting/assessment

THE WAVE REPORT—WEEKLY INNOVATION INSIGHTS

The Wave Report is a weekly column highlighting trends and lessons leaders can use to grow their leadership and their organization.

People talk about catching and riding the wave of innovation, but not many people know when and how to catch those waves, let alone understand the trends, the opportunities, and the waves as they come.

Every Friday, we send out The Wave Report, highlighting one "wave." Waves include trends or insights in innovation, fundraising, marketing, technology, and, of course, subscriptions and subscription giving.

Sign up at www.imago.consulting/wavereport to receive weekly trends and insights from The Wave Report in your inbox.

Surfs up! 🌊

Dave Raley, Founder

Imago Consulting

Sign Up for Weekly Insights and Trends at
www.imago.consulting/wavereport

CONTENTS

FOREWORD

SEVERAL YEARS AGO, I had the pleasure of sharing a meal with Dave Raley at a quirky hotel in downtown Kansas City. A few minutes into our conversation, Dave told me that he was planning to leave his large fundraising agency and start a consulting business to help nonprofits accelerate innovation and create predictable revenue. It was clear that Dave was officially ready to jump out on his own–and my immediate response was: "What the heck took you so long!" Long before we sat down to enjoy a meal together that day, I recognized that the world of fundraising desperately needed Dave's experience and wisdom. And, as his friend, I was thrilled that he was ready to share his impactful ideas with nonprofit leaders at scale.

As someone who has spent years studying and contributing to the nonprofit sector, both through my work as the CEO of Virtuous, a nonprofit CRM helping charities raise more money and do more good, and as the author of two books—*Responsive Fundraising* and *The Responsive Nonprofit*—I've seen firsthand how donor relationships can drive an organization's success. My experience working alongside nonprofits has given me a unique vantage point on the importance of donor-centric practices and innovative fundraising strategies. It's this passion for transforming the donor experience and empowering nonprofits that drives my deep admiration for Dave Raley's work.

In the ever-evolving landscape of nonprofit fundraising, few voices are as insightful as Dave Raley's. With over two decades dedicated to guiding nonprofits through the complex world of fundraising, Dave has emerged as a true thought leader for organizations striving to innovate and create financial sustainability. His deep understanding of recurring giving programs has transformed how countless fundraisers approach their work.

As a longtime friend and collaborator, I have witnessed firsthand Dave's unwavering commitment to helping nonprofits escape the trap of "lumpy revenue" and build truly predictable revenue engines. His approach is grounded in the belief that with the right strategies, nonprofits can harness the power of recurring revenue streams to fuel their missions (and maintain their sanity along the way).

The reality is that nonprofits are fundraising in a world that no longer exists. The total number of donors giving to nonprofits has consistently decreased over the past decade. Donors are more distracted than ever, and they receive a constant stream of ads and personalized messages from their favorite brands. Most donors still desire to make an impact in the world, but it's become infinitely harder for nonprofits to break through the noise. In the words of Eglantyne Jebb, founder of Save the Children, "The world is not ungenerous, but unimaginative and very busy."

In the midst of this brave new world, nonprofits have been forced to find new ways to solidify donor retention, create consistent touchpoints with donors, and mitigate the ever-rising costs of new-donor acquisition. The good news is that there's hope. The rise of the subscription economy among consumer brands has the potential to provide a template for nonprofits to fortify their retention and stay close to donors.

As American consumers, most of our extra spending money now goes toward monthly subscriptions. Netflix, Peloton, and Apple have discovered the secret to predictable growth through monthly revenue—and nonprofits now have the opportunity to lean in and leverage those same lessons for good.

Sustainable giving is more than just inspirational jargon or big ideas; it's a tactical playbook for a new era of fundraising. In a world where the subscription economy is becoming the norm, Dave adeptly connects the dots between consumer trends, shifts in US generosity, and the need for nonprofits to adapt. And he offers a road map for leveraging these insights to create recurring giving products that accelerate generosity.

For nonprofit leaders experiencing the inevitable stress of unpredictable fundraising models, sustainable giving is for you! Dave's data-backed recommendations and forward-thinking perspective offer a clear vision for how nonprofits can navigate the changing landscape of philanthropy.

Here's to the transformative insights within this book and to the continued impact of Dave's remarkable work.

Gabe Cooper
CEO, Virtuous Software and Author of
Responsive Fundraising and *The Responsive Nonprofit*

INTRODUCTION

THE DIFFERENCE BETWEEN who you are today and who you will be in five years is the books you read and the people you spend time with.

Reading a book is an investment of your most precious resource—your time. It's an investment in yourself as well, and not only in your knowledge and capabilities, although those certainly benefit, but also in helping to challenge and shape your perspective.

My friend Bobb Biehl knows a thing or two about getting the most out of a book. Over the past fifty years, he has mentored over five executive leaders and written thirty-five leadership and management tools on personal and organizational development.

Bobb suggests that any book should be read as if you are having an imaginary conversation with the author.

In some chapters, you will agree;
in others, you may disagree.
Question,
discuss, and
debate
the concepts presented.

See reading a book
like having a cup of coffee or tea
to discuss what the author has learned about the book's subject.

Just because it is in a book
obviously
does not mean it is all true or right,
any more than you can agree with whatever a friend tells you.

Who This Book Is For

The book is for nonprofit leaders, fundraisers, and anyone who cares about unleashing generosity and the opportunity for charities to build a resilient, sustainable stream of recurring revenue.

Our sector relies heavily on the generosity of everyday individuals to support the work of the mission.

As of 2022, there were 1.5 million nonprofits in the United States. Individuals comprise the vast majority of contributions, giving a total of $319 billion that year, which accounted for 64 percent of all philanthropic giving.[1]

If you are in a nonprofit and care about growing a stable stream of recurring revenue, this book is for you.

If you care deeply about generosity and are concerned about the decline in everyday giving, this book is for you.

If you have wondered how consumer trends like the subscription economy affect the way donors think about and give to charity, this book is for you.

Why This Topic and Why Now

The subscription economy has changed the landscape of recurring giving. As individuals and organizations have bought into the ongoing value of subscriptions, consumer trends have changed, and donor behavior has changed along with it. Donors are more likely to give on a recurring basis to nonprofits of all types and sizes, paving the way for a new kind of subscription giving.

While recurring giving is not new, most charities in North America have not been able to tap into this valuable source of stable funding. We'll discuss this lack of opportunity in chapter 3, the rise of the subscription economy in chapter 4, and how that has led to a new kind of recurring giving that is more accessible to all nonprofits in chapter 5.

We've studied those top-performing nonprofits tapping into this new breed of subscription philanthropy and share the core elements of building a thriving sustainer-giving program. Starting in 2023, we conducted a national study of US-based nonprofits to see what we could learn from thriving sustainer programs across the sector. Conducting interviews with leaders and reviewing benchmarks of key metrics, we combined those findings with our own experiences and interviews with other leaders to write this book.

While recurring giving is not new, most charities in North America have not been able to tap into this valuable source of stable funding.

This is not the first book about recurring giving, and given the sector's growing importance, it certainly won't be the last.

It is important to acknowledge those who came before. Specifically, I want to call out the work of Erica Waasdorp in the United States and Harvey McKinnon in Canada. They've both written no-nonsense, straightforward guides to monthly giving and have been actively working in and advancing the sector for decades.

There is truly nothing new under the sun. We all stand on the shoulders of others, and that is a beautiful thing.

Over the past ten years, some things have shifted. We've seen the rise of recurring subscriptions in every area of our personal and professional lives. Taken together, the subscription economy has shifted the way consumers purchase and experience goods and services and, in turn, has begun to reshape donor expectations and behavior.

How the Book Is Organized

The book is organized into four parts:

1. **Why Sustainable Giving Matters**—We'll review a brief history of recurring giving in philanthropy and why it is more important than ever. Then, we'll unpack three models of recurring giving programs and explain how the rise of the subscription economy has led to the emergence of a new model of sustainable giving, making it more accessible to more charities than ever before.
2. **Lessons in Subscription Philanthropy**—After establishing the importance and accessibility of subscription giving, we turn to key trends and insights learned from a national study of US-based nonprofits and an examination of the available industry research.
3. **Designing and Managing a Thriving Sustainer Program**—The book then turns to a practical guide to the key factors that lead to a thriving recurring giving program, describing key strategies and elements of the best programs.
4. **The Future of Sustainable Giving**—We conclude the book by looking forward to the trends that are continuing to shape the landscape of subscription giving and predicting how it will continue to evolve.

I see this book as waving the flag to mark a new era of sustainable giving and a field guide to use along the way.

If you don't know me, it is helpful to know my background and what has led to my passion for helping nonprofit leaders and practitioners take advantage of this opportunity.

Why Me

The first fundraising program I worked on more than twenty years ago was a monthly giving program for Union Rescue Mission in Los Angeles. Union Rescue Mission, or URM, is the oldest rescue mission in L.A. and one of the largest in the United States. I was the project manager at the mission's fundraising agency, Masterworks.

When I started, Union Rescue Mission's sustainer program was based on the concept of providing a "meal a day." Meals and shelter were the best-performing single-gift offer in fundraising for URM, so the thinking was that this would undoubtedly be the best monthly giving ask.

After struggling to grow the program and suffering from low fulfillment rates, we reimagined the program as a representative child and family sponsorship program—a monthly gift helped provide essential services for the many women, children, and families that the mission was serving on an ongoing basis.

As a monthly donor, your commitment provided desperately needed services to get these women and children off the streets and away from Skid Row, one of the most dangerous places in the country.

After reimagining the program, fulfillment rates jumped by more than 20 percent, and it immediately started to grow.

Since that first program more than twenty years ago, I've worked with, advised, educated, or inspired hundreds of nonprofit organizations and thousands of leaders.

I am passionate about helping nonprofits create profitable growth through sustainable innovation. I've been blessed to do that in a number of ways, from founding a digital team at the agency in

2006 to helping start or build teams in nonprofit fundraising across analytics, media, strategy, and innovation.

My goal is to help leaders see the the future waves of marketing and fundraising, and connect the dots to how they can take advantage of them.

One of the most important "waves" in fundraising in this generation is the shift from one-time single gifts to recurring, sustainable support driven by the subscription economy.

My goal is to help leaders see the the future waves of marketing and fundraising, connect the dots to how they can take advantage of them.

My prayer is that your investment in reading this book pays back one hundredfold as you apply the lessons here to grow your sustainable recurring giving program.

> *The difference between who you are today and who you will be in five years is the books you read and the people you spend time with.*

The quote at the beginning of this introduction is a paraphrase of a quote from Charlie "Tremendous" Jones. The original quote is, "Five years from now, you will be exactly the same person you are today except for the books you read and the people you meet."

Thank you for investing your time with me.

This book is an investment in your future self. I hope you treat it as a conversation with me over a good cup of coffee (or tea or matcha). I'm excited to share with you what I've learned. I hope you will consider, question, discuss, and debate along the way.

TAKEAWAY I've written this book to help nonprofit leaders understand how philanthropy is changing, why this presents a tremendous opportunity for hundreds of thousands of nonprofits today, and what they can do to take advantage of this new trend shaping the future of fundraising.

Also, if you want to contact me directly, my email is draley@imago.consulting.

The Rise of Sustainable Giving

PART 1

Why Sustainable Giving Matters

CHAPTER 1

Why Sustainable Giving Matters

"JANUARY 1 IS the worst day of the year."

Peter, a senior nonprofit executive, sat with Scott, a fellow leader, at a conference.

"What do you mean January 1 is the worst day of the year?" Peter asked.

"I mean," Scott responded, "that it's the worst day of the year for us nonprofit leaders because all our fundraising dashboards are reset to zero. No one cares what happened up until December 31 because we have to start all over again on January 1, raising the next year's funds almost completely from scratch."

Good job, Mr. or Mrs. Nonprofit Leader, you've worked your butt off for the last twelve months. You *hopefully* just reached your budget for the year in December. Maybe you fell short. Maybe you blew it out of the water. But guess what? It's January 1. Time to start the climb again!

That sucks.

Nonprofits the world over have felt the sting of January 1. That inescapable feeling that no matter what happened last year, here we go again.

Lumpy Income

I was two years into my career in the nonprofit world when a new vice president of development was hired at the rescue mission, where I worked as the senior account executive. Abel came from a corporate background—this was his first nonprofit fundraising job.

I'll never forget when he came to me a couple of months into the job with an epiphany. "Dave, you know what's wrong with our fundraising program?"

"And what is that?" I inquired.

"Our income stream is way too lumpy," he declared. "I've been looking at our annual results, and despite how hard we work all year, most of our income comes in between October and December, with a little bump in March/April around our Easter fundraising drive.

"Dave, what I want you to do is come up with a plan to smooth out our income."

Sure, Abel. I'd love to do the impossible is what I thought because I never would have said that to a client! But I was thinking, *Yep, that's exactly what your income stream looks like because that's what 100 percent of your peers experience too.*

Welcome to the reality for 75 percent of charities in America today—inconsistent, lumpy income, highly dependent on single, large, and often unpredictable gifts.

I had only been in the industry for a couple of years, but I had learned—and accepted—the reality that fundraising income is inconsistent. While each type of nonprofit had its seasonal patterns, revenue for most charities was anything but smooth and steady.

That conversation with Abel was in 2005. Being new to philanthropy, Abel didn't understand what fundraisers *for centuries before him* had learned and accepted—that charitable giving is inherently episodic. Uneven. Lumpy.

Abel was ahead of his time, certainly in the world of rescue missions.

In 2005, there were no good answers for how to raise consistent revenue from donors for a charity like Abel's.

Outside of a loyal handful of individuals giving monthly, the vast majority of gifts came during key fundraising periods around the Thanksgiving, Christmas, and Easter holidays.

In 2005, only 2 percent of all revenue for Abel's charity was given on a recurring basis.

Historically, nonprofits have been anything but equal when it comes to creating a sustainable recurring giving program.

TAKEAWAY One of the biggest challenges charity leaders and fundraisers face is the inconsistency of when funds come in and the unending hustle to get that next gift.

Why Sustainable Giving Is More Important Than Ever

Recurring, sustainable giving is more important than ever for several reasons.

Donor loyalty has declined for years. In 2024, after looking at giving for nearly 2,200 charities, Neon One found that the five-year retention rate for nonrecurring donors fell to 34 percent—a five-year low, down 11 percent from 2018.[2] If you extrapolate this trend over five years, then for every thousand single-gift donors acquired, *less than ten remain.*

The cost to acquire and keep a donor is rising. Costs to reach individuals on the most effective platforms are increasing.

Economic instability and consumer confidence lead to volatility in giving. Financial instability, inflation, joblessness, and even government shutdowns have all led to increasing volatility in the philanthropic sector. Giving USA publishes ***The Annual Report on Philanthropy*—the seminal publication reporting on the sources and uses of charitable giving in the United States**. The chart looks like a bad roller coaster. The 2024 report showed that inflation-adjusted giving by individuals declined by 12.6 percent between 2021 and 2022. Growth in individual giving declined by 2.4 percent in inflation-adjusted dollars between 2022 and 2023. The cumulative change in inflation-adjusted giving by individuals between 2021 and 2023 is down 14.7 percent.[3]

The number of individuals giving to charity is declining. *The Generosity Crisis*, a must-read book for anyone who cares about the state of generosity in North America, makes a compelling case for why generosity is in crisis, pointing to the decline in the number of individuals giving to charity.

On the other hand, these discouraging stats are offset by industry data reporting that regular, sustainable, recurring giving is thriving.

From 2019 to 2024, the average charity saw growth in recurring donors by 127.3 percent. —Neon One

The number of individuals giving on a recurring basis is growing. In 2024, after looking at giving over five years across 2,149 charities, Neon One found that while the average number of active donors declined by 3.5 percent, the average number of active recurring donors grew by 127.3 percent!

Sustainer Long-Term Value (LTV) is as strong as ever. The average recurring donor is worth three to nine times that of their single-gift counterparts, depending on which study you read.

Recurring giving continues to grow, even as single-gift giving declines. The 2024 *M+R Benchmarks Report* found that while one-time online giving declined by 5 percent in 2023, monthly giving *grew* by 6 percent in the same period.[4] Every study I've seen in the past three years has pointed to growth in recurring giving overall.

Recurring donors cost less to cultivate and retain. When a donor is committed to recurring giving, the organization can save the significant ongoing expense of cultivating the donor while delivering a remarkable donor experience. This isn't to say that recurring donors should not receive additional cultivation—we'll discuss this more in the book. But the cost to cultivate and retain recurring donors is lower than that of their single-gift counterparts.

Recurring donors are some of the most responsive single-gift donors. We typically see about 25 percent of giving by recurring donors in addition to their regular recurring gifts. For example, if you receive $100,000 in recurring gifts from donors, you can expect those same donors to give about $25,000 on top of their regular recurring giving.

Recurring donors are more likely to leave an organization in their will or make a legacy gift to an organization. A study in the United Kingdom found that monthly donors were six times more likely to leave a gift to the charity in their will. While similar data is not available for the United States, multiple studies point to longer-term relationships with donors leading to greater participation in legacy giving.

TAKEAWAY The cost to acquire and cultivate single-gift donors is increasing while the number of donors giving to charity is decreasing. At the

> same time, donors are choosing recurring giving more than ever before, and they have proven to be some of the most valuable, longest-retaining donors with a low cost of cultivation.

Sustainable giving is more important than ever. Yet, historically, it has not been available to the vast majority of nonprofits. But that is changing.

January 1 Doesn't Have to Be the Worst Day of the Year

Remember Peter and Scott from the beginning of this chapter? Both lamented how discouraging it was to start the scoreboard over at the beginning of the new year.

Well, Scott did something about it. Scott Harrison focused his organization's efforts on changing this paradigm. Years later, charity: water's recurring giving program, The Spring, has been a trendsetter in the sector for recurring giving. In chapter 15, we'll unpack how this singular focus on subscription giving resulted in 80,000 monthly donors and tens of millions raised to provide clean water worldwide.

And Peter Greer is president and CEO of Hope International and the author of more than a dozen books, including *Rooting for Rivals* and *The Gift of Disillusionment*. Peter was a key encouragement for me in writing this book.

As of the time of writing, Peter reports that Hope International has *doubled* the number of subscription donors in the past year, in part based on the inspiration and encouragement in discussing this book!

Incredible Opportunity and a New Wave of Accessibility

I estimate that 75 percent of nonprofit organizations in North America today are charities like Abel's—they have historically been at a tremendous disadvantage—having to reclimb the mountain of their annual funding goal each year, starting over January 1.

This has changed—January 1 doesn't have to be the worst day of the year anymore.

The question is, will your nonprofit or cause take advantage of the rise of subscription giving?

Let's do this.

CHAPTER 2

A [Brief] History of Sustainable Giving

PHILANTHROPY IS NOT new.

Simply defined, philanthropy is the use of private resources for public purposes.[5] The giving of resources like time, talent, and treasure has deep roots in human history.

The first recorded use of the term "philanthropy" was in the fifth century BC in the Greek play *Prometheus Bound*[6]—a combination of the Greek words *philos*—that which is beloved, dear, and important, and *anthrōpos*—a human being.

Philanthropy, literally translated, means *for the love of humanity.*

Philanthropy in Ancient History

In the fourth century BC, Aristotle wrote that giving money "to the right person, in the right amount, at the right time, with the right aim in view, and in the right way—is not something anyone can do, nor is it easy."

The earliest recorded bequest donation in history took place around the same time, with Plato's donation of all his land on which the Academy was founded, sometime around 350 BC.

While philanthropy was about honor and status for the Greeks and Romans, the earliest record of recurring giving in history came from a religious and ethnic group—the Jewish people.

The earliest record of recurring giving in history came from a religious and ethnic group —the Jews.

The Jewish people saw their one God as the embodiment of generosity, having rescued them from slavery to the Egyptians and given them the Promised Land. They identified the stranger, the widow, and the orphan as deserving of charity.

In Jewish tradition, the book of Leviticus states:

> When you reap the harvest of your land, do not reap to the very edges of your field or gather the gleanings of your harvest. Do not go over your vineyard a second time or pick up the grapes that have fallen. Leave them for the poor and the foreigner. I am the Lord your God. (Leviticus 19:9–10 NIV)

These acts of generosity took place every season and are some of the earliest examples of recurring giving. The Jewish practice of tithing firstfruits appears to be the earliest recorded form of recurring giving.

In the first century AD, a Jewish man named Yeshua encouraged his followers to sell their possessions and give to the poor.

These followers would later come to be known as Christians, and Yeshua would be known by the English translation of his name—Jesus.

> Sell your possessions and give to the poor. Provide purses for yourselves that will not wear out, a treasure in heaven that will never fail, where no thief comes near and no moth destroys. For where your treasure is, there your heart will be also. (Luke 12:33–34 NIV)

Later in the first century AD, a leader named Paul wrote to Christian followers in a city in Greece called Corinth:

> On the first day of every week, each one of you should set aside a sum of money in keeping with your income, saving it up, so that when I come no collections will have to be made. Then, when I arrive, I will give letters of introduction to the men you approve and send them with your gift to Jerusalem. (1 Corinthians 16:2–3 NIV)

The funds that were collected were then used to meet needs among those who had need.

> [There] were no needy persons among them. For from time to time those who owned land or houses sold them, brought the money from the sales and put it at the apostles' feet, and it was distributed to anyone who had need. (Acts 4:34–35)

In what appears to be related to the Jewish custom of firstfruits, Christians would practice setting aside funds each week, sending them in, and those funds would be used to support the poor and needy in the community.

Later on, another people of faith would prioritize charity and "put the poor and needy at the heart of its economic universe"—Muslims.

Recurring Giving and Islam

In *Philanthropy: From Aristotle to Zuckerberg*, author Paul Vallely writes that "Muslims, both rich and poor, are expected to feed the hungry, free captives and debtors, and give shelter to the orphan and the widow. It is a duty of Muslims to make sure that no one goes hungry in their community."

The concept of almsgiving is repeatedly mentioned in the Koran. Zakat is one of the five defining aspects of Islam. It is a form of mandatory almsgiving practiced by many Muslims, and the proceeds are to be distributed to the poor and the needy. Zakat is due annually, making it a form of annual recurring giving.

Islam also has a category of voluntary charity known as *sadaqah*, which is voluntary charity, and while it is at the discretion of the individual, it is associated with regular giving—"And be steadfast in prayer; practise regular charity; and bow down your heads with those who bow down (in worship)" (Koran 2:43).

TAKEAWAY: The act of philanthropy, giving on a recurring basis for the love of humanity, has been a part of human civilization dating back thousands of years.

Let's fast-forward a thousand years and examine recurring giving in the modern era and, ultimately, in North America.

Recurring Giving in the Modern Era

Recurring giving in the modern era dates back to 1698 in London.[7] Circulating a "Form of Subscription" to Anglican parishes just after its founding, the London-based Society for Promoting Christian Knowledge (aka SPCK) asked donors for a modest payment at four set times a year, through which even small donors could contribute to establishing a local charity school. In a way, this was the first form of monthly child sponsorship giving.

Recurring giving in terms of membership dates back to the advent of societies—individuals coming together to promote a cause they believed in, funding themselves through annual subscriptions from members. While philanthropic in nature, members of such societies generally stood to benefit from an exchange of value—often in the form of access or social capital with other members.

> Membership-style recurring giving originally consisted of individuals coming together to support a cause they believed in.

Unfortunately, I estimate that only about 25 percent of nonprofits have the kind of program and structure conducive to one-to-one sponsorship or membership recurring giving models. That means that, historically, the remaining three-quarters of nonprofits have been unable to significantly tap into recurring giving until recently. We'll come back to this over the next three chapters.

Philanthropy and Recurring Giving in North America

In North America, the earliest acts of philanthropy were by Native Americans. Pilgrims recorded in December 1620 the aid of a Patuxet Indian named Squanto, who served as a guide and teacher.

In what would become the United States, the earliest recorded instance of fundraising was in 1643 when three pastors conducted Harvard College's first fundraising drive, raising £500.

By the nation's founding in 1776, the roots of private philanthropy were already deep, resulting in the founding of many churches, clinics, schools, orphanages, libraries, colleges, and hospitals.[8]

The earliest documented case of one-to-one sponsorship dates back to May 24, 1815, when a group of missionaries to Bombay, India, penned a letter to the American Board of Commissioners for Foreign Mission (ABCFM) in Salem, Massachusetts. The letter proposed the concept of Christian donors "sponsoring" children while they lived in missionary homes and schools. In the ensuing months, the ABCFM wrote that the plan was "very captivating" and "contributions and communal subscriptions for this object exceed our most sanguine expectations."

In many ways, recurring giving in the United States was born on May 24, 1815, more than two hundred years ago!

TAKEAWAY: Recurring giving in the United States is not new, dating back to the nation's foundations. This book draws upon these roots and examines how things have changed, enabling a new class of nonprofits to tap into recurring giving.

Over the years, there have been three types of recurring giving, which we'll look at next.

CHAPTER 3
Three Types of Recurring Giving

HISTORICALLY, THERE HAVE been three kinds of recurring giving models.

One-to-one recurring giving is where donors are connected with beneficiaries. In this model, the donor is matched with recipients of the charity's efforts, either personally or through the charity. Common examples of one-to-one recurring giving include child sponsorship and direct staff support.

Membership recurring giving is where donors benefit from the nonprofit's programs, goods, or services. In other words, recurring donors receive some sort of value from the nonprofit—programming, content, education, discounts, access, and so on. In this model, there is an exchange of value—donors give repeatedly but receive something in return. Examples of membership-based programs include donor-supported media such as television and radio, as well as museums, zoos, educational institutions, content-based nonprofits, and so on.

Everyone Else—The final category historically has been *everyone else* left behind. These nonprofits do not have a one-to-one or membership model, leaving them with few options to create a vibrant recurring revenue stream.

There is good news, especially for this last category. Times are changing, and an entirely new class of charities is rising up that are creating resilient, sustainable, and growing recurring giving programs. We'll explore this new opportunity over the next two chapters and how to take advantage of the opportunity throughout the rest of the book.

Next, let's look at the strengths and weaknesses of the first two categories. Because if you can create a one-to-one or membership model, you should. They are powerful and can raise significant funds.

One-to-One Recurring Giving

This model of recurring giving has existed for thousands of years, and as we saw in the last chapter, in the United States, it dates back to 1815.

The donor-and-beneficiary relationship is central, and a bond forms between the giver and the receiver, making this one of the stickiest and highest-value forms of sustainer giving.

Today, the most common forms of one-to-one giving in the United States are child sponsorship and direct support of staff. In either case, the donor gives to the organization with the expectation that the individual will benefit from the support.

There may or may not be a personal relationship between the donor and recipient, and the giving often funds a broad base of programming, including direct benefit to the beneficiary.

One-to-one sponsorship is one of the strongest forms of monthly giving, typically seeing the highest retention and long-term value. If you can create this kind of program, it is a game changer.

Barriers and Downsides to One-to-One

One-to-one is not without its downsides. Donor loyalty is often more tied to the individual beneficiary than the organization or overall cause. If the beneficiary is no longer available to sponsor for any reason, it can be challenging to retain the donor.

One-to-One has also been associated with negative outcomes, patriarchalism, and imperialism. This is not to say all one-to-one giving programs lead to negative outcomes, but ignoring the implications and concerns surrounding the model would be unwise. On the other hand, if designed thoughtfully, pairing donors and beneficiaries can create community and connection and change both parties in healthy ways.

Another barrier to establishing a one-to-one model is infrastructure, which can be substantial. Programs like this require significant logistical systems, such as facilitating updates from each beneficiary to each sponsor, among other administrative burdens. Quality control can also be challenging, with many distinct relationships to maintain.

Most organizations that can offer one-to-one models like this find that the effort is well worth the reward, but there is no denying that the effort can be significant.

The biggest challenge with one-to-one giving is that the vast majority of nonprofits are unable to create a one-to-one subscription giving model. This is because the organization's program model is not conducive to connecting mass numbers of beneficiaries to donors, because of privacy concerns, or because of other issues preventing them from building such a program.

TAKEAWAY: Consider a one-to-one model if your organization has programming conducive to connecting donors directly or indirectly to individual beneficiaries. One-to-one sustainable giving is a powerful motivator for giving and an even better motivator for continuing to give.

Let's examine the next type of sustainer program where the donor is the beneficiary, at least partially—membership.

Membership Recurring Giving

The second kind of recurring giving program, membership, is marked primarily by the donor being a beneficiary, at least partially, of the nonprofit's activities. These might include goods, content, or services.

Membership giving includes any nonprofit that provides a direct benefit to the donor. That includes media organizations (donors consume content), cultural organizations such as museums, theaters, and zoos (access, discounts, etc.), education (access, social standing, influence, family members), health (services, social standing), religion (social standing, access).

In these programs, recurring givers generally give, at least in part, because of what they receive. This is not to say they pay for services, though no doubt some donors feel that way. Mostly, donors give because they value continued access ("what's in it for me") and desire to help provide access for others.

Barriers and Downsides to Membership

There are a couple of downsides to Membership giving. First, the more donors feel they are "paying" for services, the more they think and behave like consumers. They tend to expect more ongoing value and can churn at higher levels when they don't perceive value. Retention can become a challenge in these situations.

In other words, the more donors view their giving as an exchange of value, the more their giving starts to feel like a Netflix subscription and is subject to the question, "What have I gotten lately from this subscription?"

There are also the costs of creating and administrating benefits. That can be acceptable if the charity's purpose is to provide those benefits—such as educational content or programming. But creating and maintaining valuable benefits can be significant and costly.

The biggest challenge with the membership model is that the vast majority of nonprofits are unable to create a membership-style recurring giving program. Like nonprofits left out of the one-to-one model, most nonprofits do not have programming conducive to providing direct benefits to donors.

TAKEAWAY: The membership model is great for the limited number of charities that can create a valuable exchange of benefits. If that is you, a membership model can help you accomplish both program goals (e.g., education, awareness, sales or attendance, and so on) and fundraising goals (e.g., revenue, number of donors, and the like).

Like one-to-one, if you can build a membership-based recurring giving program, you should consider it.

But the vast majority of nonprofits—75 percent by my estimate—have historically fit into the third category—everyone else.

What About Everyone Else?

What about the rest of the nonprofit world?

What are they to do if they cannot create a one-to-one or Membership model for recurring giving?

Of the 1.5 million nonprofits in the United States today, I estimate that 75 percent have not been able to tap into recurring giving. That's more than 1.1 *million* charities that have been left behind when it comes to creating a sustainable stream of recurring giving funding.

But there is good news. Thanks to the subscription economy, a new model of recurring giving program has emerged.

There is hope for everyone else. There is a new model for sustainable, recurring giving.

This new model for recurring giving is so important that I've given it its own chapter. Before we turn to this new model, let's set the context by looking at one trend that has made it possible—the rise of the subscription economy.

CHAPTER 4

The Rise of the Subscription Economy

WHEN I WAS a kid, I remember eagerly waiting for my mother to finish her latest copy of *Reader's Digest.*

It may seem strange to others, but to this ten-year-old, it was like a treasure hunt. My favorite was "Word Power." Each edition would feature about a dozen obscure terms, and you had to correctly guess the meaning of each. I still remember the joy of discovery, thumbing through each issue.

Subscriptions are not new. *Reader's Digest* was founded as a subscription magazine in 1922 and, at its height, was the largest paid-circulation magazine in the world, boasting a total worldwide circulation of twenty-three million copies across forty-nine editions and twenty-one languages.[9]

A brief study of history finds the earliest publication subscriptions date back to the early 1600s.[10]

But subscriptions have dramatically changed in modern times. As Bob Dylan put it in 1964, "The Times, They Are A-Changin'."

The Rise of the Modern Age of Subscriptions

In 1999, Netflix offered its first monthly subscription. Instead of the traditional pay-per-rental model at competitors like Blockbuster Video, Netflix had a radical idea. It would offer customers unlimited rentals for $19.95 a month, delivered via mail. And with no late fees! *Innovation at its height.*

By the late 2000s, subscriptions began to gain steam. In 2013, Adobe announced a shift from a $2,000 one-time purchase for its Adobe Creative Suite software to a $49.95/month subscription. Microsoft later followed suit with subscriptions for many of its software programs. Customers were being asked to subscribe on an ongoing basis in exchange for a lower upfront cost and the promise of ongoing value.

TAKEAWAY: Today, it's difficult to find an area of our personal, consumer, and work lives that subscriptions haven't impacted.

Subscriptions Everywhere

Subscriptions impact nearly every area of our lives.

When I speak at conferences, I like to play a little game. I ask for a show of hands as I go down the following list to determine if they are subscribers.

Want to play? Your call whether to raise your hand or not—no judgment here! (If you're listening to the audiobook while driving, I recommend keeping your hands on the wheel.)

Subscriptions impact nearly every area of our lives.

Video Entertainment—Netflix, Disney+, Hulu, Prime Video, YouTube Premium

Music Streaming—Spotify, Pandora, Apple Music

Software—Microsoft Office 365, Adobe Creative Cloud, Canva, Quicken/QuickBooks, Salesforce, Hubspot, Squarespace

Subscription Boxes—Stitch Fix, Dollar Shave Club, Monthly Wine Club, BarkBox

Books—Audible, Audiobooks, Book of the Month

Apps—Apple Arcade, Google Play Pass, Duolingo, Mint

Gaming—PlayStation Plus, Xbox Game Pass, Nintendo Switch Online

Education—MasterClass, Skillshare, Coursera, Khan Academy

Fitness—Peloton, Apple Fitness Plus, Orangetheory Fitness, your local gym

News—*Wall Street Journal*, *NY Times*, *Time*, *Financial Times*, *The Atlantic*

Groceries/Meal Delivery—HelloFresh, ButcherBox, Amazon Fresh, Walmart+

Vehicles—Alternative car ownership, features like software updates, full self-driving, emergency services

Did you raise your hand? Is your arm tired?

I don't know about you, but I'm exhausted. It gets better, though—do you subscribe to your doorbell?

Subscribing to Your Doorbell

Are you subscribed to your doorbell?

When I ask this question at events, I mostly get puzzled looks. But there are always a couple of people in the audience who know *exactly* what I'm talking about because they subscribe to their doorbells too.

Over the past decade, an entire industry of video "smart doorbell" companies has emerged—Ring, Arlo, and Eufy, to name a few. These products require a subscription plan in order to access advanced features like storing recordings and "enhanced" notifications that can differentiate between a car in the driveway, a package delivery, a person, or an animal.

For example, the Ring Protect Basic plan allows footage to be retained for sixty days at $3.99/month, while the Ring Protect Plus subscription adds "unlimited" storage of footage, enables professional monitoring and cellular backup, and extends the warranty on the user's Ring products from one year to the life of the devices for just $10/month. For $20/month, Ring Protect Pro" includes 24-7 alarm professional monitoring. What a deal!

Yes, for a mere $4 to $20 a month, you can now know when your neighbor's cat walks by your front door at 1:43 a.m.—and have the video recording to prove it!

If you wonder whether video doorbells are big business, Ring was founded in 2013, and by 2018, they were doing so well that Amazon purchased the company for an estimated value of between *$1.2 and $1.8 billion*.

A decade ago, if you had told me, "Dave, in ten years, you are going to be paying *the doorbell company* $10/month for the privilege of using your doorbell," I would have said, "I don't know what this future world you speak of is, but I'm not interested!"

This used to be a fun joke I would make at conferences until it became personal. One day, my wife pointed out that she doesn't love that when I have to travel, she's home alone with the kids. She doesn't want to answer the door unless she knows who is there, Amazon packages are delivered all the time, and so on.

As of the time of writing, we've spent $566.78 on Arlo video doorbell camera equipment and paid *another* $618.49 in subscription payments.

At least now I know when the neighbor's cat is on my front porch in the middle of the night (can you tell we don't like this cat?). How I ever lived without this knowledge is hard to say.

Subscriptions are a part of our daily lives. In 2022, the average American had 6.7 subscriptions, up from 4.2 in 2019, according to Rocket Money, a personal finance app specializing in helping consumers manage their subscriptions.

95.8 percent of US adults have at least one subscription as of Q1 2023

In a related report from the Subscription Trade Association (SUBTA), 95.8 percent of US adults have at least one subscription as of Q1 2023.[11]

And subscriptions are not only everywhere, but they are good for business.

Subscriptions Are Good for Business

Subscription-oriented businesses have thrived in the subscription economy. From 2012 to 2022, subscription businesses outpaced the market (represented by the S&P 500) by a factor of almost four times.

The following chart displays the Subscription Economy Index produced by Zuora.[12] It shows compound annual growth of an astounding 16.5 percent from 2012 to 2023, versus 4.8 percent for the S&P 500 over the same period.

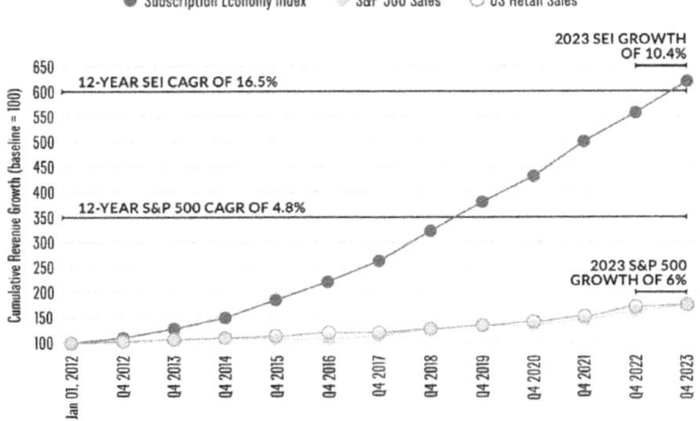

Subscriptions are thriving. The Subscription Economy Index shows that subscription businesses grew nearly three and a half times faster than the S&P 500 over the past twelve years.

The global market value of the subscription economy is expected to top $1.5 trillion in 2025.[13]

TAKEAWAY: Not only does nearly every American participate in the subscription economy, but it has also proven to be great for companies and increasingly so for nonprofits, which we'll discuss in the next chapter.

The term "subscription economy" was coined by Tien Tzuo, author of *Subscribed: Why the Subscription Model Will Be Your Company's Future—and What to Do about It.* Tzuo founded Zuora, the company that produces the subscription economy Index cited earlier.

Let's define the subscription economy before we turn our attention to how the subscription economy has led to the rise of a new model for recurring giving:

The Subscription Economy Defined

The rise of recurring subscriptions is seen in every area of consumer and business life. Customers are buying access, always-on, and anywhere, memorable experiences, ongoing value, and personalized service.

We've already established that subscriptions are in virtually every area of our lives. In part 2 of the book, we'll examine how the subscription economy is influencing donor behavior.

Let's now turn to how the rise of the subscription economy has led to a new model for recurring giving.

CHAPTER 5

Subscription Giving—A New Way

THE SUBSCRIPTION ECONOMY has paved the way, leading to the rise of a new breed of recurring giving. I call this new model subscription giving.

This is a huge opportunity for the vast majority of nonprofits that have been unable to build a thriving, growing, substantial recurring giving program.

In subscription giving, the donor is not the beneficiary, and they don't benefit from the charity's programming or services, like in a membership-based program. Likewise, donors are not connected with beneficiaries, as in a one-to-one program.

> Subscription giving programs tap into donors' desire to provide ongoing impact and providing stable support to the cause over time.

Subscription giving programs are based on the donor's desire to do good. They are shaped by an ongoing value proposition that includes alignment with the cause and providing stable, predictable support to enable ongoing impact.

TAKEAWAY: Over the past decade, we've seen tremendous growth in an emerging category of recurring giving programs that are not dependent on a one-to-one or membership model but rather a strong ongoing value proposition. We call this new breed of program subscription giving.

Examples include charity: water's The Spring, International Justice Mission's Freedom Partners, St. Jude Children's Research Hospital's Partners in Hope, and the Humane Society's Humane Heroes.

Subscription Giving Program Examples

Causes like charity: water have built recurring giving programs like The Spring based on the promise of joining a community of givers where 100 percent of giving goes to help bring clean and safe water to every person on the planet.

International Justice Mission's Freedom Partners send rescue every month to children and families trapped in trafficking and modern-day slavery. They are helping bring an end to human trafficking around the world.

St. Jude Children's Research Hospital's Partners in Hope is a special community of monthly supporters who are committed to saving children with cancer and other life-threatening diseases. They enable St. Jude to focus on what matters most—saving kids regardless of their financial situation.

The Humane Society's Humane Heroes are passionate animal advocates who have generously committed to providing reliable, ongoing support to the Humane Society of the United States. This support enables the Society to respond in emergency situations and continue fighting the root causes of animal cruelty.

We'll unpack each of these programs and the insights we can learn in part 2 of the book. But for now, it's important to note that none of these charities have a one-to-one model where donors are sponsoring beneficiaries. They aren't built around membership benefits, and outside of the occasional T-shirt or other trinket, they don't provide goods or services in exchange for recurring donations.

Yet, these recurring giving programs are strong, stable, and thriving sources of income for each of these causes, enabling them to accomplish their mission.

Subscription Giving—Sustainable Funding for Everyone Else

More than *one million* nonprofit organizations have historically been left out of the opportunity to create a strong base of sustainable giving—but not anymore.

The rise of the subscription economy has reshaped donor behavior, transforming recurring giving across the board and making sustainable funding accessible to more charities than at any other time in history.

While all nonprofits stand to benefit from understanding and leveraging the subscription economy, it's clear that these causes will gain the most in the next era of sustainable giving.

This is a massive opportunity.

"But how massive is this opportunity, Dave?"

I'm glad you asked.

The Scale of the Opportunity

In 2022, $319 billion was given to charity by individuals.[14] If 75 percent of nonprofits now have a way to tap into recurring giving and conservatively grow an additional 5 percent as a result, that could be as much as $120 billion in net new dollars over the next ten years.

And $120 billion additional to charity could do a lot—and this is just in the United States alone.

To put this figure into perspective, here are the estimated costs of solving some of the world's biggest problems:[15]

- Ending world hunger—$30 billion
- Eliminating homelessness in the United States—$30 billion
- Eradicating malaria—$8.5 billion
- Eliminating rabies worldwide—$6.3 billion
- Eradicating polio—$1.1 billion

We could fund solutions to these problems with just the net increase in recurring giving over the next ten years and *still have $44.1 billion to spare.*

What other world problems could we solve with this kind of influx of generosity?

TAKEAWAY: The emergence of subscription giving is a game changer. This is truly a "rising tide lifts all boats" moment, as all charities benefit greatly from the advent of this new third way for recurring giving.

Speaking of subscription giving, let's conclude part 1 of this book by combining all of these trends into one overarching trend—the rise of a new era of sustainable giving—subscription philanthropy.

CHAPTER 6

Subscription Philanthropy—A New Era of Sustainable Giving

AS CONSUMERS' LIVES have been reshaped by the rise of subscriptions in every area of society, donor behavior has begun to change. The subscription economy and changing donor behavior have led to substantial growth in sustainable recurring giving across the sector.

The Growth of Recurring Giving

In a 2024 study, Neon One found that the average nonprofit saw 144.4 percent growth in revenue from recurring giving over five years from 2018 to 2022. Similarly, the number of active recurring donors grew 127.3 percent over the same period. The number of donors and the amount of recurring revenue varied widely, but the growth was across the board.

Recurring giving has also proven resilient, growing even during soft times. M+R Benchmarks has conducted one of the longest-running online fundraising benchmark studies in the industry.

In its 2024 benchmarks report, M+R revealed a sobering fact—overall, online giving was down 1 percent in 2023. This came as a gut punch for many charities, following a decline of 4 percent in 2022—the first reported decline in online giving in the report's more than a decade-long history.

Recurring giving has also proven resilient, growing even during soft times.

And yet, we see a similar pattern when we look under the surface. In 2022, online giving of one-time gifts was *down* 12 percent, while monthly giving was *up* 11 percent. In 2023, the story continued, with one-time giving online *declining* by 5 percent, while monthly giving *grew* by 6 percent over the same period.

Recurring giving has become a significant pillar of the online fundraising strategy for many nonprofits, providing a reliable and predictable income stream. According to the M+R report, monthly giving represented 31 percent of all online giving in 2023—a substantial and growing amount, up from 27 percent in 2022.

Similarly, the Fundraising Effectiveness Project (FEP)—a collaboration of the Association of Fundraising Professionals (AFP) Foundation—reported declines in the number of donors, revenue, and donor retention through December 2023.[16] Overall, the number of donors was down 4.9 percent, dollars were down 6.3 percent, and donor retention was down 3.5 percent from 2022.

But once again, digging a little deeper into the Fundraising Effectiveness Project data reveals that recurring donors are more resilient. While the number of donors was down across the board, the only donor group to see growth in 2023 were donors with seven-plus donations.

The report goes on to point out that when combined with donors contributing three to six times per year, "these groups accounted for only 16.3 percent of donors yet accounted for 40.3 percent of all donations."

TAKEAWAY: Recurring donors are a growing percentage of donors and dollars in every corner of the charitable giving sector.

The Growth of Subscription-Oriented Donors

As consumers have become accustomed to the value proposition of monthly recurring subscriptions, donors have increasingly adopted monthly giving as a preferred way to give to causes they care about.

Donors are increasingly "subscribing" to give on a recurring basis to causes that are important to them.

According to Nonprofits Source, 45 percent of all donors are enrolled in a monthly giving program, with 52 percent of millennials being more likely to give monthly over a large one-time donation.

As we wrap up part 1, let's recap what we've learned.

The Rise of Subscription Philanthropy

Bringing together all of the trends we've just discussed, let's review:

The cost to acquire and retain single-gift donors has increased,

while

The number of single-gift donors and dollars continues to decrease.

while

The rise of the subscription economy has reshaped consumer behavior,

which has led to

Changes in consumer attitudes and expectations,

which is in turn

Transforming donor behavior and preferences,

resulting in

A new model of recurring giving, known as subscription giving,

leading to

A new era of sustainable giving that is accessible to more charities than ever before.

Welcome to The Rise of Sustainable Giving

Donors are increasingly subscribing to giving on a recurring basis to causes that are important to them, and smart nonprofits are leveraging the rise of sustainable giving to build and grow thriving recurring giving programs.

> Smart nonprofits are leveraging the rise of sustainable giving to build and grow to thriving recurring giving programs.

I've invested hundreds of hours over the past two years to study and understand these shifts in the landscape of philanthropy, and thousands more over the past twenty years working directly with charities to grow resilient sustainable revenue streams.

The rest of this book is dedicated to helping you take advantage of this opportunity.

Let's go.

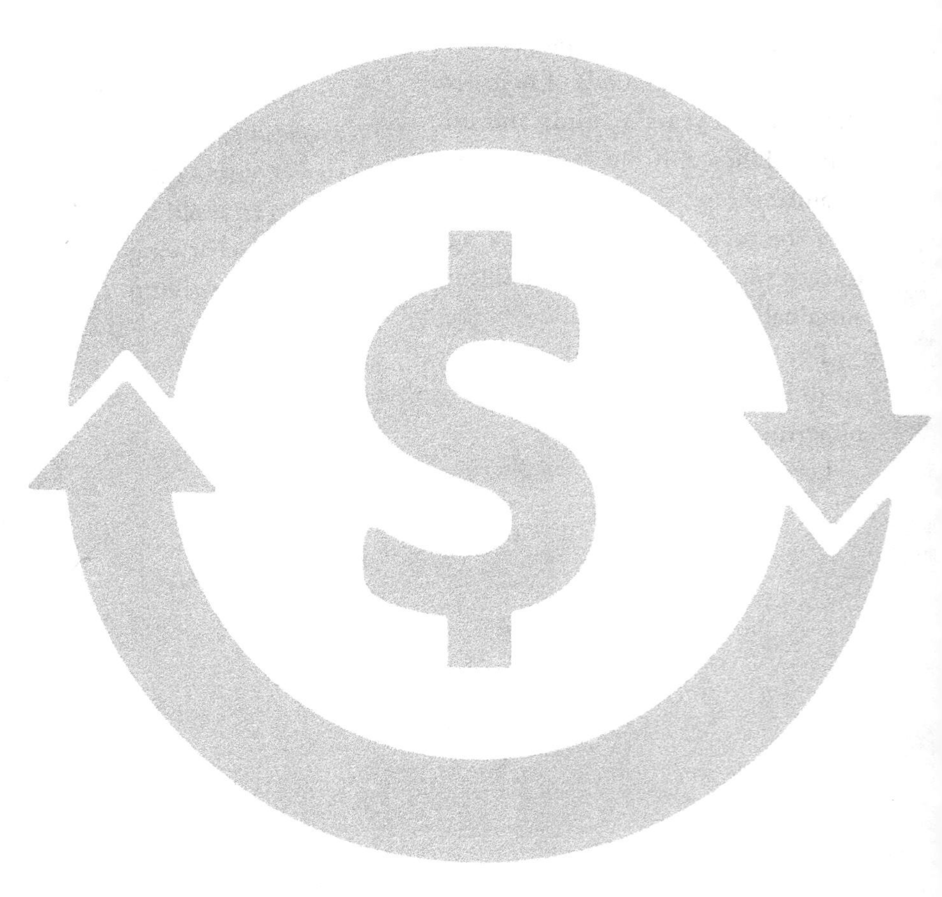

PART 2

Lessons in Subscription Philanthropy

CHAPTER 7
Setting the Stage

IN PART 1, we established the forces that have led to the rise of subscription philanthropy:

- Increased costs of acquisition and retention
- Declining single-gift donors and dollars
- The rise of the subscription economy
- Reshaped consumer attitudes and expectations
- Changing donor behavior and preferences
- A new model for recurring giving—subscription giving

These forces have let to a new era of sustainable giving accessible to more charities than at any other time in history—subscription philanthropy.

Wise nonprofits are tapping into these shifts to create and grow thriving recurring giving programs.

Part 2 of this book will look at lessons leaders and practitioners can apply to create, operate, and grow recurring giving at their organizations.

The lessons and insights outlined in the next chapters come primarily from three sources: my years of experience, a national sustainer study we've recently conducted, and secondary research into the subscription economy and recurring giving trends in fundraising.

Part two of this book will look at lessons leaders and practitioners can apply to create, operate, and grow recurring giving at their organizations.

Direct Experience with Nonprofits

Over the past twenty years, I've been blessed to work directly with more than one hundred nonprofit organizations, including human and social services organizations, international fundraising agencies, universities, faith-based nonprofits, relief and development charities, and more.

My work in fundraising, marketing, and innovation has not only focused on recurring giving; I cut my teeth in direct response marketing, starting with direct mail and traditional media. That experience was followed by nearly two decades of building or helping grow fundraising and marketing teams in digital, media, analytics, brand, content strategy, and innovation.

I've been privileged to work with many talented, highly experienced colleagues. As a senior executive, much of my time has been invested in "leading leaders"—supporting the brilliant and hardworking folks who have carved new paths forward in this sector.

I've also been blessed to be well-connected within the nonprofit community. Over the past two decades, I've been honored to speak to, train, and inspire thousands of nonprofit leaders and practitioners. As a member of the business community serving charities, I've been fortunate to learn from, advise, and cultivate relationships with many for-profit practitioners who also serve this sector.

Over the years, I've convened or facilitated dozens of groups of senior leaders and practitioners, seeking to understand the issues they face and the remarkable innovations they have developed to address those issues head-on.

But one person's personal experience can only go so far, no matter how broad. So, as I began to work earnestly on the research that would lead to this book, I looked at what we might learn from sustainer programs across the sector.

That process resulted in an ongoing national sustainer study.

Ongoing National Sustainer Study

In early 2023, we began conducting research into sustainer programs, seeking to answer one question: What can we learn across the sector from thriving recurring giving programs today?

Our research methodology includes both quantitative and qualitative elements. Each organization that participates agrees to in-depth interviews with program leadership and quantitative benchmark analysis, providing multiyear trends for metrics across ten different areas.

> We've sought to answer one question through our research—What can we learn across the sector from thriving recurring giving programs today?

We've learned broadly across the sector from charities in many different verticals, including arts and culture, environment, animals, education, health, human services, international, faith-based, and membership nonprofits.

In our research, we look for elements common across successful recurring giving programs and those unique for specific organizations.

It is fascinating to see how different types of nonprofits pursue and grow recurring giving programs differently. At the same time, the most effective programs share common denominators. The lessons we've learned are infused into the coming pages.

The final piece of the puzzle is secondary research into the subscription economy and recurring giving trends in fundraising.

Secondary Research— The Subscription Economy

I conducted a deep dive into consumer and business subscriptions to understand everything I could about how subscriptions work today. Which strategies worked and created long-term, loyal subscribers, and which strategies quickly churned through them and even damaged trust?

Understanding the impact of the subscription economy provided insight into how charities might use these trends and techniques to grow and sustain strong recurring giving programs.

I first studied companies like Netflix, Disney, Spotify, and Adobe. I read the top books in the subscription space, including the following:

- *The Membership Economy: Find Your Super Users, Master the Forever Transaction, and Build Recurring Revenue* by Robbie Kellman Baxter[17]
- *Subscribed: Why the Subscription Model Will Be Your Company's Future—and What to Do about It* by Tien Tzuo[18]
- *The Forever Transaction: How to Build a Subscription Model So Compelling, Your Customers Will Never Want to Leave* by Robbie Kellman Baxter[19]

Then I interviewed people like Robbie Kellman Baxter, author of *The Membership Economy* and *The Forever Transaction: How to Build a Subscription Model So Compelling, Your Customers Will Never Want to Leave.* Robbie is the nation's leading expert on subscriptions and has worked with companies in over twenty industries, including Netflix, the NBA, the *Wall Street Journal*, and Microsoft.

I also interviewed Amy Konary, founder and chair of the Subscribed Institute at Zuora—the company that coined the term "subscription economy." Amy is a pioneer in the world of subscriptions, credited with coining the term "Software as a Service," or SaaS—one of the most successful categories of subscriptions over recent years.

I poured over data and research from leading subscription companies like Zuora, ProfitWell, and Recurly. Understanding the trends in the subscription economy has proved invaluable for this book.

The final source for data and insights into subscription philanthropy comes from the nonprofit sector.

Secondary Research—Recurring Giving Trends

While there is no publicly available set of consistently calculated data on recurring giving, various research has been published on the topic, fortunately.

Here is a brief review of some of the resources available in the space. This book will not attempt to capture all of the data, strategies, and points of view. I would encourage you to access and review these different sources for yourself.

I want to give special thanks to Erica Waasdorp, A Direct Solution, who regularly maintains a curated list of the research available on recurring giving at www.adirectsolution.com/monthly-donor-statistic.

Following is a list of major sources that I'll reference throughout this book.

Provider/Source	Summary
M&R Strategic Benchmarks 2024[20]	Online fundraising benchmarks across types of giving.
The Recurring Giving Report 2024—Neon One[21]	Data and five-year trends on recurring giving from 2,149 nonprofits.
Dataro Benchmarking Report 2023[22]	Global fundraising trends based on 68 million donations from 117 organizations.
Classy's State of Modern Philanthropy 2022[23]	Annual report combining data from fundraising platform Classy and parent company GoFundMe data on 34 million donors and over $5 billion donated.
Blackbaud Luminate Online Benchmark Report 2022[24]	One of the original online fundraising reports, based on 653 organizations online giving of $1.5 billion.

Provider/Source	Summary
Blackbaud donorCentrics Sustainer Summit Benchmarking[25]	Data through FY2023 of top sustainer fundraising organizations participating, from 37 organizations representing 20 million donors and $3.3 billion.
ECFA State of Giving 2023[26]	Data on the past 10 years of giving to churches and Christian nonprofits.
NextAfter's Recurring Giving Benchmark Study[27]	2018 study documenting how 115 nonprofits treated donors around recurring giving.

Each of these resources provides a window into the grander narrative of recurring giving today, and while recurring giving is not always the main focus of the research, they still provide insights into the state of recurring giving.

TAKEAWAY: The insights in this book are a combination of my own experience working with and speaking to hundreds of nonprofits, our ongoing national study of sustainer programs, and secondary research in both the business of subscriptions and nonprofit trends in recurring giving.

Subscription Philanthropy—The Future of Sustainable Giving

My direct experience working with charities, the ongoing national study, and a deep dive into the research available on the subscription economy and the state of sustainer giving today paint a picture of recurring giving going through a metamorphosis.

That metamorphosis is the rise of subscription philanthropy, a new era of sustainable giving that is more accessible to more charities than at any other time in history.

My goal is to help you see the lessons you can draw from this transformation and apply them to your context.

Let's start by looking at six key shifts driven by the subscription economy that you can apply to grow subscription giving.

Subscription philanthropy is a new era of sustainable giving that is more accessible to more charities than at any other time in history.

CHAPTER 8

Six Key Shifts Driven by the Subscription Economy

IN CHAPTER 4, we established that the rise of subscriptions has impacted nearly every area of our lives, that it has led to unprecedented participation in ongoing, recurring relationships with companies' products and services, and that it has been good for business and consumers alike.

But what exactly can nonprofits learn from the subscription economy that you can apply directly to building resilient, stable, recurring giving programs?

In this chapter, we'll look at critical shifts driven by the rise of subscriptions and how charities can tap into each.

Six Key Shifts from the Subscription Economy

Robbie Kellman Baxter is one of the world's leading experts on subscriptions. She is the author of *The Forever Transaction: How to Build a Subscription Model So Compelling, Your Customers Will Never Want to Leave.* Over the past twenty-plus years, she has worked with organizations like Netflix, Intuit, Fitbit, Microsoft, the *Wall Street Journal*, and *Consumer Reports*.

Robbie and I have had multiple conversations about how she's seen the landscape of subscriptions change over the past nearly twenty years she's been in the space. When she started, companies didn't see the opportunity with recurring revenue. Today, she says "Every board is telling their leadership team, we have to have recurring revenue."

In her book, *The Forever Transaction*, Kellman Baxter writes about the rise of subscriptions leading to several shifts for consumers and membership businesses:

> It means moving from an ownership model to one of access, from a single payment to multiple recurring payments, from an anonymous transaction to a known relationship and from one-way—or even two-way—communication to a full community gathered under the umbrella of the organization.
> —Robbie Kellman Baxter, *The Forever Transaction*

In this excerpt, Baxter identifies four fundamental shifts brought on by the subscription economy:

- From an ownership model to one of access
- From a single payment to multiple recurring payments

- From an anonymous transaction to a known relationship
- From one- or two-way communication to community

Based on our research, I've added two more shifts and rearranged the order to reflect how these changes have specifically impacted generosity and recurring giving.

1. From **transactions** to **engaging experiences** (*mine*)
2. From **ownership** to **access**
3. From **anonymous** buyers to **known** customers
4. From **periodic interaction** to **ongoing value** (*mine*)
5. From **single purchases** to **recurring payments**
6. From **one- or two-way communication** to **community**

Let's unpack these shifts in turn and discuss how charity leaders can tap into each.

Subscription Economy Shift 1: From Transactions to Engaging Experiences

Subscriptions create engaging experiences that go beyond the transaction—experiences of discovery and delight.

Spotify is a perfect example of a subscription that goes beyond the simple transaction of "renting music." One reason that today I'm happy to send Spotify $16.37 a month is because of the surprising, engaging experience of discovery.

How might your charity cultivate engaging experiences for sustainers with your organization and with the cause?

As I write this chapter, I'm listening to Spotify. The streaming service has learned what kinds of music I like, and

I'm regularly delighted when it introduces me to a new artist or song I've never heard of but perfectly fits my taste. Just yesterday, Spotify played a song for me called "Welcome to Wonderland" by an artist named Anson Seabra. It's a beautiful tune by an artist I had never heard of before, and it was a delightful experience. With one click I was able to create a streaming radio station of music based on this one song and artist.

The best subscriptions provide a remarkable, engaging experience. Sometimes, those start with a free version, but in every case, the company knows that one way to convert and keep subscribers is to continue to provide an exceptional experience.

How might your charity cultivate engaging experiences for sustainers with your organization and with the cause?

I remember when we became Freedom Partners, the sustainer program for International Justice Mission. My wife, Heather, was at an event in Dallas called the IF:Gathering. The event organizers had partnered with IJM to tell the story of the work the organization does to fight human trafficking. It was a moving conversation, and Heather stepped forward to commit to their recurring giving program, Freedom Partners.

That was eight years ago. Other than missing one month due to a new credit card being issued, we've given every month since then. Our family has given $2,609 as of this writing, all via small gifts at low cost to IJM—and all because of this powerful experience more than eight years ago!

TAKEAWAY: The best subscriptions move beyond the transaction to create an engaging experience. Nonprofits that understand the power of experience can leverage that to create powerful moments that delight and inspire recurring donors.

How can you create powerful, engaging experiences around your sustainer program? We'll talk more about identifying and creating powerful moments in chapter 22, but for now, consider what experiences could be the most delightful and engaging for your constituents.

The next shift the subscription economy has seen is the transition from ownership to access.

Subscription Economy Shift 2: From Ownership to Access

Subscriptions deliver value by providing ongoing access.

The ability to gain access has proven to be a powerful ongoing value proposition for subscribers. Sticking with our Spotify example, as a subscriber, I value accessing content anytime, anywhere, and on any device. I regularly switch between streaming music via Spotify on my laptop, iPhone, children's iPads, and our Amazon Echo. I can also download music to play offline when I'm on a plane without internet access or even in another country.

How might your charity provide access to your recurring donors, whether to exclusive content, relationships, community, or other ongoing value?

Another form of value where subscriptions can provide access is in experiences not available to everyone, discounts, or limited products as a member.

For nonprofits, access can mean making content available to sustainers that is not widely available to others. It can also mean access to experiences or individuals they might not otherwise have. Likewise, some nonprofits can offer discounts or access to insider updates.

How might your charity provide access to your recurring donors, whether to exclusive content, relationships, community, valuable discounts, or other offerings?

TAKEAWAY: The shift from ownership to access has become a key source of value for subscriptions. Likewise, nonprofits that can provide access to recurring donors can create value for their most faithful supporters.

One of the most powerful shifts driven by the subscription economy is the one from anonymous buyers to known customers.

Subscription Economy Shift 3: From Anonymous Buyers to Known Customers

Subscriptions create value through a deeper experience enabled by knowing customers.

How can you tap into the direct relationship you have with recurring donors to personalize and tailor their experience?

Before subscriptions connected them directly, customers were largely invisible to companies. The relationship went through some sort of intermediary (a distributor, retailer, media channel, etc.).

Subscription relationships directly with customers not only result in better profit margins for businesses but also enable them to get to know their customers. When the customer sets up a subscription with the company in question, a direct relationship begins. The most successful brands tap into this known relationship by tailoring and improving the product and experience based on that knowledge.

Netflix doesn't just have data on the kinds of entertainment that are popular—they know *exactly* what kinds of entertainment *you* like. Their ability to then tailor that experience to the things you are interested in makes the ongoing value proposition significant.

When brands know their subscribers, it empowers a virtuous cycle—the more the individual uses the subscription, the better and more tailored the subscription becomes. This is possible because customers are known to the subscription companies.

In the nonprofit sector, we've long had a direct relationship with donors. But we can learn from how subscription businesses continuously tailor and personalize the experience to individual donors' passions and interests.

How can you tap into the direct relationship you have with recurring donors to personalize and tailor their experience? What can you communicate to show that you know them? How might you delight them by customizing the experience based on data you might have about them? That data might be a birthday, a specific type of program they have a history of supporting, an extra gift to a previous appeal, or any number of other individualized data points.

TAKEAWAY: Subscriptions have enabled a new world of possibilities to tailor product experiences to provide enhanced value. Nonprofits can tap into this trend by considering ways to personalize the journey and generate increased value for donors and charities alike.

The critical moment in the journey to subscription is when the ongoing value exceeds the friction of acting.

Subscription Economy Shift 4: From Periodic Interaction to Ongoing Value

Subscriptions go beyond occasional benefits to providing ongoing value.

The tipping point for many subscriptions is when the value created becomes a habit, delivering benefits in an ongoing way. This ongoing value outweighs the friction of the cost of the subscription, whether that is monthly, annually, or another frequency.

> How might your charity articulate your value proposition in a way that justifies giving on an ongoing basis?

Pandora, and later Spotify, nailed this ongoing value proposition for me. Starting with a free, ad-supported version, I used the tool until it became a daily habit of listening to music—while I worked, when traveling, at a coffee shop, or in my car. The delight of being introduced to new artists and access to the world's music was so compelling that the value of eliminating ads and having more features (like skips and listening anywhere) outweighed the friction of paying for such a service. So I subscribed.

Pandora was the first subscription music service I ever paid for. In this case, the point of conversion to recurring payments happened late in the journey, after the value was already being received.

For nonprofits, the central question is how might you articulate your value proposition in a way that justifies giving in an ongoing way? We'll delve into the topic of crafting an ongoing value proposition in the next chapter.

TAKEAWAY: Subscriptions require an ongoing value proposition that exceeds the friction of signing up. Similarly, the value proposition for ongoing giving must justify the ongoing relationship and go beyond taking the best single-gift offer and asking for "twelve of those" a year.

Where the rubber hits the road is when the subscriber or donor makes the decision to become a recurring supporter of the cause and moves from single gifts to recurring payments.

Subscription Economy Shift 5: From Single Purchases to Recurring Payments

The customer decides to move to an ongoing, automated, recurring payment in exchange for value.

Note how late in my musical discovery journey I decided to sign up for recurring payments. When I speak about the subscription economy, audiences naturally assume one of the first things I will talk about is the shift to recurring automated payments. Some assume that recurring payments are pretty much all there is to the subscription economy.

> Does your nonprofit make the sign-up and checkout flow for becoming a recurring donor smooth and effortless?

Hopefully, by now, you see that there is so much more to the shift to ongoing subscriptions than the mechanics of payment processes. Before any customer is willing to commit to an ongoing payment relationship, they need to believe that they will have an engaging experience and ongoing access, be known as a customer, and receive ongoing value. Only then will they be ready to subscribe to recurring automated payments and wish to stay subscribed.

Subscriptions are predicated on providing so much ongoing value that the consumer is willing to sign up for recurring payments.

While the payment process step comes later in the value journey than most people tend to think, it is no less important. Signing up for automated recurring payments should be seamless and easy and instill confidence—that the individual's data will be secure, processed in a timely manner, and easily managed.

Nonprofits thankfully have increasingly better technologies and tools available to make the donor experience more akin to the subscription customer experience—but we still aren't entirely there. For example, many nonprofits are not able to do some or all of the following:

- Enable recurring donors to manage their giving online securely and easily
- Pause giving for a defined period of time
- Give donors access to see all of their giving history in one place.

We'll discuss this in more detail in part 3 of this book—in chapter 27 on the recurring giving tech stack and in chapter 29 on retaining donors and minimizing churn.

TAKEAWAY: The decision for a customer or a donor to take action to set up a recurring automated payment only happens after the perceived value of that payment is justified. Consider how your charity can help potential recurring donors see a glimpse of the ongoing value proposition.

Let's turn to the final shift the subscription economy has seen—the shift from one- or two-way communication to community.

Subscription Economy Shift 6: From One- or Two-Way Communication to Community

Subscriptions are increasingly becoming the conveners and facilitators of community.

One shift I would not have naturally guessed is that subscriptions are increasingly becoming the gathering places for connection and community.

Users of subscription products gather at conferences, conventions, and virtual spaces. For example, designers, photographers, and others gather at Adobe Max, billed as the "creativity conference," or Hubspot's Inbound, the gathering place for practitioners in the field of inbound marketing. Other more fan-oriented gatherings include Blizzcon, the annual gathering for fans of various games developed by the company Blizzard, like World of Warcraft, Diablo, Hearthstone, and more.

These events bring together thousands of people with shared interests and passions, who naturally form communities.

However, subscriptions' role in facilitating connection and community extends beyond events and gatherings. Subscription services like Spotify increasingly play a role in connecting people with the subscription itself.

Spotify enables the creation and sharing of custom playlists with friends. In effect, one can create entire radio stations for themselves and their community. Others can subscribe to these playlists, curated by the community. For example, I've created a dynamic playlist for my two daughters called "For My Sweet Girls." I regularly add songs that Spotify suggests that I think they would appreciate. It's drawn us closer as it causes me to think about them and we connect through a shared love of music.

Then there is Spotify Wrapped, which has taken the community aspect of the subscription experience to another level. Spotify Wrapped is a hyperpersonalized summary of a subscriber's last year of listening habits, generating engagement through sharing with the community.

> How might your nonprofit convene and cultivate a community of donors passionate about your cause?

Each December, Spotify prepares a summary of the listening habits of each listener, recapping last year's tastes and guilty music pleasures. Spotify Wrapped is a "celebration of the year gone by and an invitation to join in on the fun." Each holiday season, social media feeds are filled with posts of people reflecting on the year that was, illustrated by the music and themes they listened to most. Social media feeds light up each December as people proudly share, connect, and laugh about their different musical preferences of the year.

When subscriptions play a role in enhancing our connection and community, they become even more valuable, and, I would add, they become even better for humanity.

Charities can take cues from subscriptions that tap into the power of convening and connecting the community of individuals around a shared passion. Causes have historically been the convening place for community, and charities have an ongoing role to play in facilitating connection.

TAKEAWAY: Subscriptions increasingly play a role in connection and community, which charities can naturally tap into as they have historically been the gathering place for people passionate about a shared interest.

When I asked Robbie what advice she would have for nonprofits looking to tap into recurring giving in the subscription economy, she said, "Understand what your goals are and why you're doing it before you launch into your experiment. Be patient. It takes longer than you think to figure it out. Don't jump to conclusions that if it doesn't work right away that it doesn't work in your market. It's a different culture—membership is very much about the long-term relationship."

The Role of Charity in the Six Shifts

The rise of the subscription economy has led to six fundamental shifts that charities can and have learned to tap into as they build resilient, sustainable recurring giving programs. Let's recap and consider the role of charity in each of the six shifts.

1. From **transactions** to **cultivating engaging experiences** with your organization and with the cause.
2. From **ownership** to **special access** to information, people, and experiences that donors would not otherwise have to the cause.
3. From **anonymous** donors to **known individuals** who receive a personalized and tailored experience.
4. From **periodic interaction** to providing **ongoing value** that fosters continued engagement and support.
5. From **single donations** to ongoing **recurring giving**.
6. From **one- or two-way communication** to **nurturing a community** of people passionate about the cause.

In the next chapter, we will examine how a nonprofit organization can translate these six shifts into recurring, subscription giving by developing an ongoing value proposition.

CHAPTER 9

Subscription Giving Requires an Ongoing Value Proposition

ONE OF THE biggest changes brought about by the rise of the subscription economy is the importance of an ongoing value proposition. With a subscription, the value received needs not only to exceed the cost but also to be received on an ongoing basis.

With a subscription, if the value stops, then subscribers cancel and churn.

One of the mistakes I see fundraisers make regarding recurring giving in the old paradigm is treating subscription giving as interchangeable with single-gift fundraising. In essence, they see recurring giving as simply a one-time gift offer that just happens on a regular, automated basis.

A subscription is as much about cultivating ongoing value as it is about acquiring the subscriber in the first place. So it is with subscription giving—the first hurdle is to get the donor to commit to recurring giving. The second hurdle is providing them an experience with ongoing value such that they continue to give.

As we will discuss in chapter 10, the most important metric in subscription fundraising is long-term value. Because of this reality, consumer subscriptions know that the race is just beginning when they get a new subscriber. It's a marathon, not a sprint.

Consumer Subscriptions and Ongoing Value

In today's subscription economy, consumers quickly drop or add subscriptions if they are not providing ongoing value.

The 2023 Subscription Commerce Industry Outlook study found that while 95.8 percent of all US adults have at least one subscription, consumers are more discerning about which subscriptions they have. They are more readily willing to cancel subscriptions that do not provide ongoing value or switch to competitors with a better value proposition.

In fact, *52.6 percent of US adults canceled a streaming service subscription in 2023*. Take that in for a second. Over *half* of Americans were ready and willing to drop a streaming subscription if it didn't provide ongoing value.

At the same time, 59.8 percent of US adults *added* a subscription to a streaming service. In other words, subscriptions are much more sensitive to cancellation—and addition—in the consumer world. It's all about ongoing value.

TAKEAWAY: Consumers are ready and willing to cancel subscriptions that don't add value and are just as likely to add them. It's all about the ongoing value proposition.

Thankfully, donors are more loyal than consumers. If you are a nonprofit, your subscription giving donors should be more resilient than the typical subscriber.

But the reality is that people are more willing to drop or add monthly commitments than ever before, conditioned by the subscription economy.

Amy Konary, founder of the Subscribed Institute, has been a pioneer in the subscription space, credited with coining the term software as a service (SaaS), an industry standard today. She encourages nonprofits to "think about it as a start-up within your own business and really taking the principles of customer centricity and future proofing to heart." Customer centricity requires an ongoing value proposition, and future proofing recognizes that today, subscriptions evolve and change on an ongoing basis.

> Keeping subscribers—like keeping donors—is about providing ongoing value.

TAKEAWAY: Subscribers are more ready and willing to drop and add subscriptions than ever before. Keeping subscribers—like keeping donors—is about providing ongoing value. In my experience, donors are more resilient than consumers regarding recurring giving. However, we can still learn from subscription businesses about the centrality of an ongoing value proposition to keep and upgrade your subscription donors.

Consider the transition from owning music to subscribing to a streaming service like Pandora or Spotify. The value proposition had to go beyond "renting music." By itself, the fact that you were paying monthly for music was not the thing that caused Spotify to reach 226 million paying subscribers.

Spotify had to develop an ongoing value proposition. In their case, that value proposition includes the following:

- A delightful, engaging **experience** of discovering music
- **Access** to a vast library of music anytime and anywhere
- A **personalized** experience based on deep knowledge of its customers
- **Ongoing value** first established through a free ad-supported service, then later by spending hours using the product daily/weekly
- Accumulated value such that customers are willing to sign up for **recurring payments**
- A sense of being a part of a shared **community** of people connecting over music

Spotify understands that its customers' value is tied directly to the ongoing value they get from the service. That's why they keep paying, and that's why they have high value to the company.

> Like subscriptions, recurring giving needs a value proposition that justifies ongoing engagement.

Like subscriptions, recurring giving needs a value proposition that justifies ongoing engagement. It needs to make sense to the donor. The same things that might justify a single purchase are different from those that cause a customer to subscribe month in and month out.

A compelling value proposition for ongoing recurring giving needs to make sense on an ongoing basis. Why do you not just need a single gift, but how does my gift make a difference every month? What need would cause me to feel good as a donor about my ongoing impact?

What's your ongoing value proposition for those giving on a recurring giving to your cause?

CHAPTER 10

Understanding Donor Motivation

THE DECISION TO commit to giving to an organization on a regular recurring basis is a significant one. It's not as easy and low effort as a one-time donation, which is often given in the moment and based more or less on impulse—particularly for small gifts.

To maximize donor engagement, conversion, and retention, it's essential to understand donors' underlying motivations so you can meet them where they are.

Knowing why donors give to you is always important, but it is even more so when asking for a regular recurring commitment to giving. Sustainable subscription giving is a more significant ask than a single, one-off gift.

Sustainable subscription giving is a more significant ask than a single, one-off gift.

Understanding Donor Motivation is Key

Allen Thornburgh is principal and executive director at Sublimity, a studio that uses human-centered design to help faith-based nonprofits create experiences that move people to action. Over the past several years, Allen and his team have designed and launched several successful sustainer programs using a specially created form of human-centered design.

I first met Allen over a decade ago when he was the vice president of marketing for Prison Fellowship, the world's largest Christian nonprofit organization for prisoners, former prisoners, and their families, and a leading advocate for justice reform. I later had the privilege of working with Allen at Masterworks, an agency that specializes in working with faith-based nonprofit organizations.

Allen introduced the concept of human-centered design, which was first popularized by the design and consulting firm IDEO—a firm famous for inventing the original computer mouse.

Thornburgh saw an opportunity to tap into the practices of human-centered design for charities. Human-centered design is a concept popularized by the design and consulting firm IDEO. Allen told me, "I wanted to help organizations learn how to create remarkable new experiences that really mattered and could help accelerate and launch their organization."

Harvard Business School defines human-centered design as "a problem-solving technique that puts real people at the center of the development process, enabling you to create products and services that resonate and are tailored to your audience's needs."

When it comes to recurring giving programs, Thornburgh says, "Sustainer programs are just one of those types of relationships with your audience that has to be exceptional. Your sustainer program has to be remarkable. It has to enchant your audience."

"You have got to be able to find a way to translate that into a powerful experience. Quantitative data just can't really help you with that, frankly."

Allen and his team use a process of interviewing donors at three separate stages to understand donor motivation and inspire sustainer programs.

1. Source
2. Focus
3. Launch and Iterate

The first stage is source. "That's where we're sourcing insights and ideas. We get great hypotheses from the organization and great insights and ideas from the audience members."

The process involves interviewing donors in a particular way, using long-form, in-depth interviews to glean insights into their underlying motivations for giving, what fuels their imagination, and their best and worst experiences with giving.

The team then takes these insights and co-creates potential sustainer program concepts with the charity and then puts those concepts back in front of donors in a second stage, called focus.

In the focus stage, they work with the charity to turn the insights gleaned from the source stage into multiple concepts. "We turn those into concepts, and we test those concepts with audience members and get their reactions to them."

On the importance of reviewing the concepts with donors, Thornburgh says, "We take the audience members through each stage of the journey and discuss what gaps there are in that journey, and there typically are some."

The final stage is to launch and iterate.

The team reviews the final concept and revises it until they can move forward with building out an MVP, or minimum viable product, of one concept. This MVP, a quick version of the program they create in a couple of months, enables the team to further test and refine the program in the market before rolling out and expanding it.

Before using this approach, the sustainer programs that were designed and launched succeeded about half the time—a decent track record for innovating new giving programs. However, after implementing a human-centered design methodology to understand donor motivation and designing programs based on those insights, Allen's team saw a double-digit increase in successful program launches.

If you understand donor's motivations and tap into them, you will be more likely to create a better recurring giving program, which is critical for sustainable giving.

Returning to my interview with subscriptions expert Robbie Kellman Baxter—when I asked Robbie for one piece of advice for nonprofit leaders, she shared, "They should be thinking about why somebody would want to be part of a recurring program. Why would a donor or a participant want to? What's in it for them? And I think there's a lot of ways to look at it, but you have to start with what brought them here in the first place, why do they stick around, and who are they?"

TAKEAWAY: Understanding donor motivation is critical to developing and maintaining a successful subscription giving program, and the best way to uncover that motivation is through talking with donors themselves.

Next, let's establish that subscription giving is more than a simple fundraising offer—it's a full-fledged program.

CHAPTER 11

Subscription Giving Is a Program, Not an Offer

ONE OF THE most foundational elements in fundraising is the concept of a fundraising offer, but recurring giving involves so much more than a strong offer.

The simplest definition of an offer I've heard comes from Steven Screen at the Better Fundraising Company:[28]

> **Offer: a simple description of what your donor's gift will accomplish.**

A good offer includes the following elements:

1. The problem or opportunity
2. How the nonprofit is addressing it
3. How much it will cost
4. How the donor can be involved

5. A timeline that evokes a sense of urgency
6. The consequences of not acting (implied or declared)

More Than an Offer

One of the biggest mistakes nonprofits make when investing in growing their subscription giving program is treating recurring giving as "just another" fundraising offer. They think of a recurring gift as being nearly the same as a single-gift offer—another "arrow" to add to their quiver of fundraising offers.

> One mistake nonprofits make when investing in growing their subscription giving program is treating recurring giving as "just another" fundraising offer.

The problem with this thinking is that it implies a couple of things:

First, treating recurring and one-time gifts the same implies that the offer alone is enough. If we package the right need, present it to donors, and ask for a monthly commitment, they will respond.

Second, it implies that organizations can use the same strategies and tactics as single-gift fundraising. If direct mail works when asking for one-time gifts, just swap out the offer and send direct mail with a monthly ask instead; voila, you get monthly donors!

Unfortunately, it's not that easy. Anyone who has tried to take a traditionally single-gift channel like direct mail and swap in a monthly giving offer already knows how difficult it can be to make that work.

Subscription giving is not the same as taking a single-gift offer and asking donors for "twelve of those" a year.

Case Study—Union Rescue Mission on Why Subscription Giving Is More than an Offer

As I mentioned in the introduction to this book, the first nonprofit I ever worked with on a monthly giving program was Union Rescue Mission in Los Angeles. Union Rescue Mission, or URM, is the oldest rescue mission in Los Angeles and one of the largest in the United States. Founded in 1891, the Mission exists to bring help and hope to men, women, and children experiencing homelessness in and around downtown Los Angeles.

URM's first monthly giving program was based on taking their very best single-gift offer—meals—and turning it into a monthly giving program. The idea was that for about a dollar a day—the cost for the mission to provide a meal for homeless people—donors could support the work of the mission.

The best single-gift offer was providing a hot meal and shelter for people experiencing homelessness. Since the cost of a meal was a little more than one dollar, a donor could provide thirty meals—or a meal a day—for about thirty dollars a month.

Intuitively, the program made a lot of sense at the time. The concept of a meal-a-day monthly giving program was born.

> Subscription giving is not the same as taking a single-gift offer and asking donors for "twelve of those" a year.

The problem was that the program eventually stalled out. It was stuck at several hundred donors. It also suffered from low retention and fulfillment.

After stepping back and considering the kinds of work that the Mission did that might be conducive to a monthly giving offer, the decision was made to shift from the meal-a-day offer to a representative child sponsorship program.

We redesigned the program to focus on the increasing number of women, children, and families coming to the shelter, often through no fault of their own. Each month, for thirty dollars, a donor could provide resources and critical care. Donors would receive a story of a different family or woman and child each month, including a picture (representative, to protect privacy). The picture could be displayed on a calendar they received at the beginning of the year, showing the cumulative impact of their ongoing giving.

The program humanized the impact of the donors' giving and helped them see the changing face of homelessness in Los Angeles.

After the new recurring giving program launch, fulfillment rates immediately increased by more than 25 percent. This was very encouraging, especially in the days when check writing was still a significant part of monthly giving. This resulted in a significant increase in revenue immediately, and the program began growing again.

The rapid growth in the program was due to a few key insights.

First, while the best single-gift offer was good at getting one-time gifts, it could have been more effective at convincing donors to give monthly or keeping them giving monthly.

Second, giving to provide a meal is less emotionally "sticky" than giving to a person. For donors giving monthly to provide a meal a day, if you missed a donation, it wasn't a huge deal. But by shifting the focus to giving to support people—in this case, a representative child—donors felt a lot more personal responsibility not to miss that monthly gift. By cultivating a human connection with need, donors would be more likely to fulfill that commitment.

Third, the program tapped into a unique need that the organization was facing at the time—the unprecedented rise in the number of homeless women and children coming through their doors each day.

Finally, it enabled the URM team to treat the growing program increasingly independently of the day-to-day single-gift fundraising program. They were able to communicate with and cultivate monthly donors separately, sending them specially tailored communications and reducing the number of single-gift appeals. They acknowledged and affirmed those donors through personalized copy, tailored thank-you letters, and a special annual calendar with pictures of the representative children they had helped support throughout the year.

TAKEAWAY: Recurring giving is not the same as your best single-gift offer, just twelve times a year. Your best one-time ask likely is not the same as the best recurring donor ask. The value proposition for monthly giving is different and should provide ongoing value.

Like successful subscriptions employ a holistic approach, thriving sustainer programs go beyond a simply articulated offer.

While the fundraising offer is essential and should present an ongoing value proposition, the offer is just one part of an overall system that thriving sustainer programs employ. In other words, an offer alone is not enough.

Ten Areas of a Thriving Sustainer Program

A full-fledged sustainer program consists of ten interconnected fundamental components. Part 3 of the book will discuss each of these and provide best practices, but for now, we'll list and describe each.

1. **Program Design**—The recurring giving program includes a clear brand identity, an offer that justifies ongoing involvement, impact at different price points and ask amounts, benefits, and a dedicated presence in all channels.

2. **Structure & Team**—An internal structure that supports growing a thriving recurring program, including clear ownership, budget, a long-term investment mindset, and allocated resources appropriate for the program's stage of growth.
3. **Systems and Platforms**—Processes and technology that provide the foundation for an effective and growing program, including back-end technology, front-end tools, and middleware critical to the subscription giving tech stack.
4. **Acquisition**—Attracting new donors whose first gift is recurring. It typically takes a powerful offer or a well-known organization or cause to convert new donors to recurring. These new donors commit to giving on a recurring basis right out of the gate and form the basis for recurring giving for many nonprofits.
5. **Conversion**—Growing recurring donors and revenue by converting existing one-time donors to give on a recurring basis. The other side of the coin from acquiring new recurring donors is converting existing donors to give on a regular basis.
6. **Cultivation**—When donors choose to give to an organization on a recurring basis, that marks the beginning of a new phase of the relationship, not the end. Cultivation includes onboarding new recurring donors, creating powerful moments, and cultivating donors for the long term.
7. **Upgrading**—One of the greatest missed opportunities for charities today is cultivating relationships with recurring donors that lead to increased value. This includes traditional upgrades of recurring gift amounts and additional single gifts and nontraditional ways of increasing value, including middle- and major-donor prospecting and planned giving.
8. **Retention and Cancellation**—The value of a recurring donor is primarily determined by how long they remain with

the organization, so retention and cancellation prevention strategies are very important.

9. **Reactivation**—Once a donor stops giving on a recurring basis, several strategies can be considered to continue cultivating that lapsed sustainer.
10. **Measurement**—How we measure recurring giving should look a lot more like how subscription-oriented businesses measure their performance than many single-gift-focused nonprofits. Metrics like long-term value (LTV), churn, monthly recurring revenue (MRR), annual recurring revenue (ARR), and net payback are critical.

TAKEAWAY: Creating subscription giving is about having a holistic approach to creating a program rather than just focusing on a single great fundraising offer.

One final issue with treating recurring giving like "just another offer" is that it leads to a lack of internal ownership at organizations and, even worse, a lack of resourcing to grow the program. Let's tackle that next.

CHAPTER 12:
The Value of Clear Ownership

HAVE YOU EVER been a part of a group project where no one took the lead?

As a kid, I remember seeing old black-and-white clips of the famous comedy duo Abbott and Costello. They were doing a sketch called "Who's on First." Do you know it?

First made famous by the duo in the 1940s, "Who's on First" is a classic—often considered one of the greatest comedy routines of all time. The skit opens with Bud Abbott asking his partner Lou Costello, "How do you like my ball club, Lou?"

Lou responds that he'd like to know some of the guy's names on the team. Bud replies, "Sure, I'll introduce you to the boys, but they give them funny names, Lou."

Bud starts in, "Let's see, Who's on first, What's on second, I Don't Know's on third …"

Lou interrupts. "Are you the manager?"

"Yep."

"You know the guys' names?"

"I should."

"Then tell me the guys' names."

"Of course," Bud replies. "Who's on first . . ."

"But you said you knew the guys' names."

"I'm telling you their names."

"So tell me their names."

"Who's on first, What's on second. . ."

"So who's on first?"

"That's right."

"What?"

"No, What's on second!"

The next five minutes are hilarious. Lou gets increasingly angry at Bud's apparent lack of knowing Who's on first, What's on second, and I Don't Know's on third. I highly recommend watching it. Search YouTube for "Abbott and Costello–Who's on First."

The Abbott and Costello skit was way before my time, but it's as hilarious as it is relevant today. Who's on first? What's on second? I Don't Know's on third?

Some days, organizational leadership can feel this way. When there is no clear owner, no person who feels ultimate accountability, things can devolve quickly into a game of "Who's on First?"

When there is no clear owner, no person who feels ultimate accountability, things can devolve quickly into a game of "Who's on First?"

The consequences of a lack of a clear owner are especially painful for subscription giving. Everyone gives their opinion, but no one owns decisions. Teams are unwilling to make hard choices. Individuals are evaluated on short-term metrics like revenue and number of new donors and not long-term subscription giving. And perhaps most crucially, no one person feels the accountability and pressure to ensure the project or initiative is successful.

TAKEAWAY: When a lack of clear ownership and responsibility exists in subscription giving programs, it hinders the health and growth of the entire program.

Consequences of a Lack of Ownership in Subscription Giving

There are six significant consequences that stem from a lack of clear ownership around recurring giving.

Consequence 1: The Sustainer Program Gets Lost in the Shuffle

When recurring giving is treated as just one of many giving programs and no one feels any particularly deep sense of responsibility for it, other priorities can easily take over.

It can feel like there is always a bigger fire to put out or a more pressing task. I think this is partly because of the longer-term nature of recurring giving programs. While the benefits from sustainer programs almost always happen in the short term—less than twelve months—it takes consistent discipline not to be pulled away by the constant call of other urgent tasks.

It can feel like there is always a bigger fire to put out or a more pressing task.

Whether organizations realize it or not, this is a major problem for charities. For example, I often see recurring giving being lumped together with single-gift-focused direct-response fundraising as a shared responsibility. The same teams responsible for maximizing single-gift fundraising are responsible for monthly giving. Without clear ownership, sustainer giving gets lost in the shuffle.

Consequence 2: Without Ownership, Recurring Giving Loses to Competing Priorities

It is easy for the program to lack any sense of significant priority if no one "owns" the program and feels a sense of personal accountability.

Everyone on the team is doing their job, and if recurring giving is not clearly owned or is only a small part of someone's plate, then it won't be advocated for at the needed level.

Healthy organizations regularly wrestle with competing priorities, especially when investing "the next best dollar." When a sustainer program lacks an advocate, losing to other competing priorities is easy.

The strategies and tactics of recurring giving can conflict with other programs, such as single-gift direct-response fundraising, so it should not be a surprise when the program is bumped aside without a dedicated advocate.

When everybody's partly responsible, nobody feels the personal pressure and accountability to make tough decisions in the interest of growth.

Consequence 3: Tough Decisions Aren't Made

In situations where no one feels personal responsibility for the sustainer programs, it's common for tough decisions not to be made.

Team members are happy to voice their opinions and concerns, but tough decisions go unmade. This lack of decisiveness occurs, especially if the decision involves uncertainty and risk.

For example, there are often windows of time in the fundraising calendar that would be better focused on a subscription giving campaign. But doing so would require replacing or significantly changing a single-gift-focused campaign. Even if more value might be generated by the new strategy, there is always risk, and changing what has been the typical approach is a tough decision—one that someone needs to advocate for.

When everybody's partly responsible, nobody feels the personal pressure and accountability to make tough decisions in the interest of growth. It's just easier not to make a decision.

When there is no clear ownership, goal setting most often reflects whatever channel or strategy it is associated with.

Consequence 4: Goals and Metrics Are Misaligned and Misunderstood

Just like subscriptions require different metrics and measurements, sustainable recurring giving requires its own set of measures. But when lumped together with other fundraising programs, two problems arise.

First, recurring giving suffers from being measured by a scorecard that is fundamentally not set up to track the health of a subscription-style ongoing program. Instead, the most common measures and metrics are tailored to track one-time giving and emphasize measures like response rate, net revenue, short-term ROI (return on investment), and cost per gift. These metrics are not completely irrelevant to sustainer giving but are not tailored to an ongoing recurring program and lack other key metrics such as monthly recurring revenue (MRR), churn, and long-term value (LTV). We'll look more deeply at the metrics around recurring giving programs in chapter 21.

The second issue is that recurring giving suffers from misaligned goals. When there is no clear ownership, goal setting most often reflects whatever channel or strategy it is associated with.

For example, suppose a recurring giving program is lumped in with a single-gift direct response program. In that case, there might be goals around cost per acquisition or short-term ROI that are not only not helpful but counterproductive to making good decisions about the program's growth. When responsibility and accountability are lacking, there is no one to challenge and correct these misaligned metrics and goals.

In addition, fundraising agencies that serve nonprofits also often get caught in this trap, with their performance being measured almost exclusively on short-term, single-gift-centric metrics. How you measure and reward your partners shapes what they focus on and what they are able to do.

You know how painful it can be if you've ever been judged by the wrong standard or held to misguided goals. You also know how hard it is to set the record straight and get the scoreboard to reflect the right kinds of metrics and goals.

Consequence 5: Resourcing Is Not Properly Allocated

Clear ownership enables awareness of needs, understanding where the next best dollar should be invested, and advocacy for the resources to do the job.

When no one is clearly responsible for recurring giving, subscription giving goes under-resourced.

Clear ownership enables awareness of needs, understanding where the next best dollar should be invested, and advocacy for the resources to do the job.

Resourcing includes both the people, time, and budget to do what needs to be done, and when there is a lack of ownership, it's no wonder many recurring giving programs are underresourced.

If you have any doubts about whether you might be under-resourcing your recurring giving program, look at what percentage of your revenue comes from monthly giving and compare that to the percentage of time, attention, staff, and budget you allocate to that program. Are they even close?

So far, each of the consequences we've discussed points to one final trend prevalent in subscription giving—a lack of accountability.

Consequence 6: A Lack of Accountability

If everyone is accountable, then no one is. Like Costello asked Abbott, "Who's on first?" we are all seeking clarity, and clear ownership is one way to establish clarity.

If everyone is accountable, then no one is.

The central theme of this chapter is accountability. When no one feels personal accountability for recurring giving within an organization, the program's health and growth suffer.

As we've just seen, resourcing is not properly allocated, goals and metrics are misaligned and misunderstood, tough decisions often go unmade, the program loses to other priorities, and it can get lost in the shuffle.

Let me share an example of this in action, and then we'll look at ways to create a sense of responsibility and accountability around your recurring giving program.

World Vision and the Power of Accountability

The year was 1983, and Steve Woodworth was an up-and-coming analyst on the marketing team. Over the prior several years, the organization had seen healthy growth in its monthly giving child sponsorship program.

Steve was looking for a new challenge, and leadership at the time had a hunch. You see, once a new child sponsor came into the program, no one person was responsible for these recurring donors. This may seem crazy today, but the thinking was that once a child sponsor had been acquired, the hard work was done. Sponsors were then handed off to the donor services team to handle fulfillment.

While the donor services team was responsible for onboarding and managing the sponsor relationship, leadership hypothesized that if they put someone in charge of sponsors, they might see improvements in retention, giving, and long-term value.

They asked Steve to take on the responsibility. He accepted and was the first person in the organization's history to be accountable for the retention and growth of sponsorship from 1983 onward, even as his career grew to become head of marketing for the entire organization in 1988. Some of the early breakthroughs that came from having a marketing person owning sponsor cultivation include the following:

- Testing revealed that sponsors should receive fewer direct mail appeals than they had been receiving. The frequency of asking for extra gifts was hurting retention. Longitudinal testing uncovered the optimal number of appeals to be six per year—far fewer than before.
- Targeted appeals were developed, acknowledging appreciation for what the sponsors were already giving. One

particular appeal stood out, asking sponsors to sign an enclosed Christmas card and return it to be forwarded to their child. The appeal generated a staggering 50 percent response rate and millions of dollars in its first year. Other "bounce-back appeals" were developed, increasing sponsor giving dramatically.

- A lapsed sponsor series of mail and phone calls was tested and optimized, resulting in much higher retention of sponsors.
- A monthly "billing" system was developed and tested, resulting in better retention that became another multimillion-dollar breakthrough.

In just the first few years that Steve ran the sponsor cultivation program, sponsor giving nearly doubled.

Accountability matters!

No Matter the Structure, Accountability Is Key

In our research and my experience, there is no one right structure for a recurring giving program. It often depends on various factors, such as the size of the organization, donor file, channels used, and the program's maturity.

At least one person must feel accountable to advocate for the health and growth of recurring giving. As we'll see next, for some organizations that might be a senior executive over an entire team, with different aspects of recurring giving falling under the ownership of

At least one person must feel accountable to advocate for the health and growth of recurring giving.

different individuals. For others, it's a shared responsibility; for still others, it's the mantle of an "advocate" of the program internally.

But one thing is clear—a single individual who feels a sense of accountability is important. Without that accountability, the issues I've just outlined will show up, and your program will not grow as much as it could or should.

Structuring Recurring Giving in Your Organization

Some organizations hold this level of accountability to the most senior executive responsible for the program. This is appropriate and good but comes with a caveat. Sometimes, that senior-most executive has so many programs under their "accountability" they have to defer to their lieutenants. They may be "accountable" in the sense of being a senior executive, but they are not "responsible" because they will directly lead and ensure the program's success. In this case, it's important that accountability cascades to the next layer of leadership, as you might for any other significant fundraising program.

Other organizations cannot assign any one person to be solely responsible for the program. In those cases, appointing an advocate is the next best thing—someone with whom the central responsibility of the program lies.

Another approach I've seen organizations take with some success is appointing an outsider to be responsible for the program. This outsider can be either a consultant or an agency. If this approach is to be successful, it's important that subscription giving is a priority for leadership and that that partner has clear ownership and accountability to grow the program and the resources to do so.

Many Structures, One Accountability

I've done my best here to avoid prescribing a specific structure, as no one arrangement stood out in our research as the ideal.

The one thing that is common among the healthiest and fastest-growing sustainer programs is a sense of ownership and accountability. This sense of ownership and responsibility can come via dedicated staff, vendor/partner involvement, an internally appointed advocate, or a combination of all three.

There is a recognition that ongoing recurring giving is not the same as single-gift fundraising or any other fundraising program, so it should have dedicated ownership.

TAKEAWAY: It's essential to have a clear "owner" for recurring giving—someone with accountability and responsibility for advocating for the health and growth of the program—and the resourcing to make it so.

Speaking of clear ownership and accountability, let's next look at what we can learn from the discipline of product management for subscriptions to apply to recurring giving.

CHAPTER 13

Product Management and the Four P's of Subscription Giving

IN THE SUBSCRIPTION economy, product management is considered essential to driving the success of subscriptions.

Robbie Kellman Baxter, the author of *The Forever Transaction*, says, "The product manager is probably the most important and strategic hire of any subscription business—they are the person who puts together all the parts of the subscriber experience and creates something that delivers on the organization's 'forever promise.'"

The product manager is probably the most important and strategic hire of any subscription business

Product management is understood to be so crucial to the growth of subscriptions because subscriptions are products too.

Kellman Baxter explains, "It's critical to remember that the initial offering is just a starting point, and that the minimum viable product (MVP) is just the minimum. How the organization continues to evolve that offering over time to stay true to that promise, and deliver increasing value against that promise, is what guarantees you a long and mutually beneficial relationship with each subscriber."

In the world of recurring subscription giving, it's important to recognize that we are not dealing with a simple one-time fundraising offer, but a holistic program. Because of this, we need to think about managing sustainers as an entire product discipline.

TAKEAWAY: Product management is a discipline that charities would do well to leverage as they seek to grow their subscription giving program.

As we design subscription giving products, a concept I find helpful from the world of marketing and product development is called the "four *P*'s" of marketing. Let's look at that next.

The Four P's of Subscription Giving

In the world of marketing and product development, the concept of the four *P*'s has been around for decades.

I first learned about the four *P*'s as a marketing major in college. Introduced in the 1950s by Neil Borden, an advertising professor at Harvard, Borden popularized the idea of the marketing mix, which would later be known as the four *P*'s by E. Jerome McCarthy in 1960:[29]

1. Product
2. Price

3. Place (or Distribution)
4. Promotion

Far too often, marketing is confused with the last *P*—promotion, which is to promote your product. However, real marketing goes far beyond the simple promotion of a product via advertising, public relations, or communications. Marketing also includes bringing the right *product* to market with the right *pricing* strategy, distributing it in the right *places* to maximize exposure. And, yes, marketing includes *promoting* the product as well.

Let's unpack this concept by looking at each *P* and how it relates to subscription giving.

Product—What Is It, Who Needs It, and Why?

The website Investopedia summarizes the four *P*'s well, starting with product, the first *P*.[30] "Creating a marketing campaign starts with an understanding of the product itself. Who needs it, and why? What does it do that no competitor's product can do? Perhaps it's a new thing altogether and is so compelling in its design or function that consumers will have to have it when they see it."

> Recurring giving is a holistic product, not a simple fundraising offer.

What does your subscription giving program do for donors and beneficiaries? What kind of value can it offer donors? What are the benefits, intangible or otherwise? Does it make sense why it needs to be ongoing, and will it hold donors' imaginations?

TAKEAWAY: Recurring giving is a holistic product, not a simple fundraising offer. Consider what it is, who it is for, why they would "subscribe," and what they get.

Price—Connecting Value to Impact

"Price is the amount that consumers will be willing to pay for a product. Marketers must link the price to the product's real and perceived value while also considering supply costs, seasonal discounts, competitors' prices, and retail markup."[31]

> There are many ways to price a subscription giving program

How is your recurring giving program priced? Is it based on a fixed per-unit price based on impact, like thirty-eight dollars sponsors a child or forty dollars provides clean water? Or do you encourage donors to set the amount based on how you guide them? Is there a minimum ask amount? What are the incentives (things like matching donations or premiums or special insider updates)?

In addition, if a nonprofit sells tangible goods or services, discounts can be a great thing. While most nonprofits may not have traditional pricing tools like discounts, other price incentives like matching gifts or donated goods multipliers exist. All of these things contribute to increasing the value of the giving commitment to donors.

TAKEAWAY: There are many ways to price a subscription giving program—fixed per-unit pricing, open asks, and example impacts. In addition to pricing, there are other tools that can help drive value for donors—matching gifts, multipliers, or incentives.

Place—Getting in Front of the Right People at the Right Time

"Place is the consideration of where the product should be available—in brick-and-mortar stores and online—and how it will be displayed."[32]

Another word for *place* in product marketing is *distribution*. How do you get your product where your customers are? For a consumer product, that might mean buying premium placement on physical store shelves or in the checkout line.

> Placement of your recurring giving program is key to growth

Where are you putting your subscription giving product in front of potential and current single-gift donors? Is it front and center on your website? Featured at events? Included in single-gift donor and volunteer onboarding? During tours of your programs? In receipt packages? In partners with corporate partnerships? And so on.

TAKEAWAY: Placement of your recurring giving program is key to growth, just as it is for product purchase and subscription. The more prominent and targeted your placement to the right would-be donors in the right contexts and at the right times, the more effective your recruitment efforts will be.

Promotion—Communicating the Whole Package

"The goal of promotion is to communicate to consumers that they need this product and that it is priced appropriately. Promotion encompasses advertising, public relations, and the overall media strategy for introducing a product."[33]

The last area where subscription marketing and donor subscription giving marketing overlap is in the need to communicate the product via communications, advertising, media, and public relations.

How do you communicate subscription giving to potential and existing donors? Consider your paid advertising efforts in social, digital, and search. Consider organic efforts such as content marketing, SEO, organic social, and PR. Consider email and offline channels such as phone, face-to-face, direct mail, TV, and radio.

TAKEAWAY: Promotion is the last mile—communicating the program to would-be subscription donors. Promotion ensures that prospective and existing donors are aware of the subscription giving program and ultimately drives awareness, conversion, and growth.

> Promotion is the last mile—communicating the program to would-be subscription donors.

In the era of sustainable giving, cultivating a healthy, thriving sustainer program requires going beyond a simple offer. A strong subscription giving program incorporates a holistic consideration of the product, price, placement, and promotion.

Next, let's look at the most important, yet the most misunderstood, metric in fundraising—long-term value.

CHAPTER 14

It's All about Long-Term Value

LIKE SUBSCRIPTIONS, THE true power of recurring giving is the snowball of accumulated value that builds over time. It's the law of compounding at work. Financial gurus talk about the power of compounding returns over a long period. Subscription giving is the power of compounding for charities.

Of the most successful subscription businesses, Robbie Kellman Baxter says, "The organizations that have done the best have balanced three metrics—acquisition, retention, and *customer lifetime value*, and are constantly considering how each of those is doing and which one, if any, is out of balance. That's the secret to longevity."

If I offered you the choice between two donors:

- Donor A gives $2,155 annually
- Donor B gives $941 annually

Which would you choose?

I'm sure you already sense this is a trick question. Why would anyone choose Donor B, who is giving less than half their counterpart?

With no other information, any smart fundraiser would choose Donor A and take that extra $1,214 to the bank.

But let's say we introduce a couple of new data points.

- Donor A has a churn rate of 66 percent and will, on average, stay with your charity for 1.7 years.
- Donor B has a churn rate of 23 percent and, on average, will stay with your charity for 7.7 years.

Now, which donor do you want?

Donor B, of course. Over 1.7 years, Donor A gives $3,663.50. But Donor B is resilient, giving for 7.7 years for a total of $7,245.70—nearly twice as much!

And you guessed it—Donor A is a single-gift donor, and Donor B is a recurring subscription giving donor.

This is real donor data from 2,149 nonprofit organizations, included in Neon One's 2024 Recurring Giving Report. It reinforces the power of recurring giving over the long term.

Long-Term Value, or LTV, should be the most important metric in all of fundraising.

A quick note for the rest of this chapter—long-term value is also referred to as LTV, and because "LTV" is easier to write and say, we will use that more often than not going forward.

The Most Important Metric—Long-Term Value

The most crucial metric in recurring giving and arguably in all of fundraising is LTV.

Long-term value and its sibling, long-term net income, are valuable for several reasons:

- **Predictability**—Understanding the long-term value of donors enables nonprofits to predict future revenues more accurately. This predictability helps in planning and sustaining long-term projects.
- **Growth**—Focusing on LTV encourages strategies that foster donor retention and loyalty, leading to a more stable and growing funding base.
- **Efficiency**—Acquiring new donors is often more expensive than retaining existing ones. By maximizing LTV, nonprofits can optimize their spending by focusing on retaining and cultivating relationships with current donors.
- **Resource Allocation**—Knowing the LTV helps in better allocating resources toward high-value donors who are more likely to contribute significantly over time.
- **Loyalty**—Cultivating long-term relationships builds trust and loyalty, which can lead to increased donations, bequests, and other forms of support.
- **Strategic Planning**—Understanding LTV provides valuable data to inform strategic decisions, such as marketing approaches, donor engagement strategies, and program development.
- **Stewardship**—Effective stewardship of high-LTV donors leads to more net income to accomplish the charity's mission, higher satisfaction, and a greater likelihood of continued support.

> Long-Term Value, or LTV, should be the most important metric in all of fundraising.

TAKEAWAY: Long-term value is the most important metric in all of fundraising and should weigh heavily in all decisions around subscription giving.

With all of these great benefits, it's unfortunate that sustainer long-term value is the most misunderstood and underutilized metric in fundraising.

Why is LTV the most misunderstood and underutilized metric in fundraising? The first reason is that there is no consistent definition of LTV for sustaining donors.

Long-term value is the most misunderstood and underutilized metric in fundraising.

No Consistent Definition of Long-Term Value

In our research, one thing stood out when benchmarking metrics for sustainer programs—there is no consistent definition of LTV.

To illustrate this, consider your subscription giving program. Assuming you are connected with a charity and that you track long-term value, how does your nonprofit calculate the LTV of its recurring donors?

- What time period do you use?
- Do you include *all* gifts from recurring donors or *just* recurring gifts?
- Are quarterly, biannual, or annual recurring gifts included?
- Do you calculate LTV for single-gift donors differently than how you calculate it for recurring donors?

- Is LTV a projected metric based on past behavior or a reflection of actual results?
- Do you use gross revenue or net income?
- If you use net income, does that account for just the cost of acquisition or the cost of cultivation as well?
- Do you track cost per sustainer?

Different time periods. Different decisions regarding what counts. Apples-and-oranges comparisons with single-gift donors. Different rules lead to differing assumptions, which lead to different decisions.

This mixed bag of rules and assumptions around LTV makes benchmarking an exercise in frustration and prevents charities from truly understanding the health of their subscription giving programs.

The first major problem with long-term value is that there is no consistently agreed-upon industry-wide definition of the metric.

This lack of consistency contributes to a second, even more significant problem—LTV is not incorporated into short-term decision-making.

LTV Not Incorporated into Day-to-Day Decision-Making

LTV is not used to actively allocate budgets or set priorities. This means that the most important metric in fundraising rarely impacts these critical decisions.

This absence of long-term value quietly reinforces a short-term mentality. If leaders judge day-to-day performance on short-term metrics only (conversions, gifts, clicks, average gift, cost per acquisition), they are bound to make decisions that are biased toward the short term.

Spoiler alert—sustaining gifts rarely "win" in the short term.

- Average gift amounts are lower.
- Acquisition and conversion rates are lower.
- Cost to acquire is higher.

If gift amounts are smaller, conversion rates are lower, and cost is higher, why pursue a recurring donor at all?

The answer is long-term value—that's why. LTV is the gift that keeps on giving.

The power of a sustaining gift is what happens month after month, year after year—as we've seen, sustainers retain at much higher rates than their single-gift counterparts.

When I talk about long-term value at conferences, it's common for heads to nod in agreement. Leaders intuitively understand that performance over the long term is important, or at least they've heard enough about "investing for the long term" that it rings true.

The challenge comes when we have to use LTV to run our programs.

TAKEAWAY: LTV lacks a consistent sector-wide definition and is not used in day-to-day decision-making, severely limiting its effectiveness as a tool to grow subscription giving.

The first step to making progress toward using LTV on a day-to-day basis is to establish a standard definition for long-term value. Then we need to incorporate it into decision-making.

Developing a Consistent Definition of LTV

Over the years, I have talked to many leaders and seen a variety of approaches to LTV, including some very nuanced and clever definitions. It's important to keep our definition simple. LTV is going to be hard enough to find because it requires multiple years of data, so using complicated statistical models will make a common definition impractical.

In the interest of keeping the definition straightforward and widely useful, here's a proposed definition for the calculation of LTV:

LTV = 60-Month Total Giving from Donors

Let's break this down:

Sixty-Month—This five-year window is long enough to incorporate the natural accumulation of value that we want to understand of any donors, without being prohibitive to calculate. Any donors who drop off along the way will be naturally incorporated—if a donor makes two gifts and lapses after ten months, that will be accounted for in a sixty-month window, just as the donor who gives for a full five-plus years.

Total Giving—All giving from donors is included, not just specific types of gifts, such as recurring gifts. This includes monthly, biannual, or annual recurring gifts, upgrades, and any one-time gifts. Including all gifts is critical because recurring donors are one of the best sources of additional single gifts. These are typically the organization's most committed donors, so we need to account for all the value generated by their participation. Note—we do not include legacy gifts here, but we recommend tracking when recurring donors do give legacy gifts.

From Donors—We are talking about individual donor records. This is pretty straightforward—there isn't much else to say here.

You might be wondering why I haven't included retention rate, churn rate, average gift, or other metrics in my proposed definition of LTV. The beauty of a sixty-month window of all giving is that these metrics naturally blend into LTV.

Likewise, when calculating single-gift donor LTV, we should use the same sixty-month window for all giving. Due to the nature of single-gift giving, most donors will fall off at some point before sixty months, which again will be naturally reflected in the calculation.

TAKEAWAY: Charities can create a simple, consistent metric to judge performance by using a sixty-month window of all giving from recurring donors as LTV.

But defining long-term value and building LTV into ongoing reporting and day-to-day decision-making is a different matter. Let's turn to that now.

Incorporating Long-Term Value into Decision-Making

The next step to making decisions based on LTV is to ensure that it's included in every report and analysis of performance.

LTV in Acquisition

It is a mistake to compare upfront metrics for single-gift acquisition to sustainer acquisition or conversion. They are apples and oranges—response rate, average first gift, cost per acquisition, ROI—all will be very different.

It is a mistake to compare upfront metrics for single-gift acquisition to sustainer acquisition or conversion.

For example, a typical response report for single-gift acquisition includes metrics such as the following:

- # Sent/# Impressions
- # Gifts
- Average Gift
- Revenue
- Cost
- Net Income
- ROI

These metrics are short-term—they reflect what happened today, for now. To incorporate a long-term view, simply add two metrics:

- Projected Long-Term Value (LTV)
- Projected Long-Term ROI (LT-ROI)

Based on history, what is your projected LTV of the donors acquired or converted? And based on that LTV, what is the long-term ROI on the cost of the campaign?

By adding these two metrics, you'll immediately benefit from decision-making from a longer-term perspective. For example, here is a hypothetical campaign comparison of single-gift acquisition to recurring donor acquisition:

	Single-Gift Campaign	Recurring Campaign
# Gifts	100	25
Average Gift	$53	$33
Revenue	$5,300	$825
Cost	$8,800	$8,800
Upfront ROI	0.6	0.1
Projected LTV	$23,850	$28,875
Projected LT-ROI	2.7	3.3

If decisions are based on short-term metrics like response, revenue, and average gift, recurring donor efforts can look like poor investments. Only when you incorporate long-term value can you see the true return of subscription giving.

In the previous example, if I were looking only at the typical short-term metrics, the recurring campaign would look like a failure. Who wants to run a campaign with a 0.1 ROI?

Once LTV is incorporated, however, we see a different picture. These donors who give consistently are worth significantly more to the organization because they give month in and month out.

TAKEAWAY: Incorporate LTV into acquisition reporting and decision-making to ensure a balanced view of the fundraising program's long-term health.

The next element of incorporating LTV into day-to-day decision-making is retention and upgrade strategies.

LTV in Retention and Upgrade Strategies

If the value of a recurring donor is largely about what happens after the first gift, then it logically follows that our metrics and strategies should focus on subsequent giving: onboarding, extra gifts, upgrade asks, lapsed prevention, cancellation, and reactivation.

In part 3 of the book, we'll cover both strategies for retention and increasing the value of recurring donors. For now, it's important that LTV be included in retention and upgrade performance reporting, most commonly in donor file health dashboards.

TAKEAWAY: Incorporating LTV metrics into donor file health, particularly retention and upgrade performance, helps leaders extend their perspective beyond short-term acquisition into the long-term onboarding, cultivation, and upgrading of donors.

Finally, LTV should be central to the practice of financial forecasting, budgeting, and evaluation.

LTV in Forecasting, Budgeting, and Evaluation

LTV should be included in strategic and budget planning. Better decisions are made when prioritizing, planning, and projecting with long-term value incorporated.

While it pays off today, the bulk of the value in subscription giving is experienced year after year. In the world of consumer subscriptions, subscription companies have a multiyear investment mindset. Nonprofits would do well to learn from this.

> In the world of consumer subscriptions, subscription companies have a multiyear investment mindset.

Budget cuts are common to recurring giving programs because "we can't afford to wait for a long-term payback." But remember that recurring donors give more annually than many single-gift donors. A $33/month subscription donor who retains at 78 percent gives an average of $309 annually versus a $53 single-gift donor who gives 1.7 gifts a year for $90 annually. That's a short-term payback.

Investments in subscription giving donors pay back this year, not just over the long term!

Finally, it's critical that LTV be included in program and team evaluation. If LTV is the most important metric, then performance evaluations should incorporate it.

TAKEAWAY: To properly understand, prioritize, and grow subscription giving, organizations must have a consistent definition of the long-term value of subscription donors, report on it at all levels, and include it in evaluations. Remember: long-term value doesn't do you any good if you don't use it.

> Investments in subscription giving donors pay back this year, not just over the long term!

Long-term value helps leaders understand the actual value of a strategy by zooming out and asking, "What is the return over time?" LTV helps avoid pursuing short-term gains at the expense of long-term losses. It helps create resilient funding programs that compound upon themselves. It naturally blends key metrics that contribute to LTV, such as average gift, gift frequency, longevity, and churn.

Let's now look at a trend that has increasingly emerged as leaders have caught a vision for the power of a long-term, predictable, efficient, and growing source of sustainable funding—sustainer-first fundraising.

CHAPTER 15

Sustainer-First Fundraising

IN OUR RESEARCH, we noticed a pattern among some of the most successful programs. This pattern wasn't universal, but it certainly is present in large and small organizations alike and appears to be growing.

Increasingly, charities are leading with recurring giving. For these charities, their sustainer program is given prominence. Other gift types are welcomed, but the implication is undeniable—our best, most loyal donors who are making a difference for the cause are giving on an ongoing recurring basis.

> Increasingly, charities are leading with recurring giving.

This trend goes by different names, like "sustainer first," "sustainer primary," or "sustainer forward." But it includes organizations like World Vision, Compassion International, the Humane Society of the United States, and charity: water. These organizations all have had periods of, or are still, almost exclusively focusing on recurring giving.

Charities like St. Jude's Children's Research Hospital and the Humane Society of the United States default donation forms to monthly frequency with messages like "St. Jude kids depend on you" and "Save all animals year-round!"

For organizations like World Vision and charity: water, the sustainer-first mindset goes very deep.

World Vision and its Core Driver

World Vision is one of the largest charities in the world. In 2023, the organization reported $1.5 billion in revenue. Their impact has been tremendous—in 2023 alone, they distributed 208,000 tons of food supplies, helped establish access to clean water for 3.1 million people, improved sanitation for nearly 2.5 million, and equipped 2.9 million with household handwashing facilities, responded to seventy-eight humanitarian emergencies in fifty-nine countries, distributed 9.6 million bed nets, and distributed nearly $800 million in microloans, impacting nearly 1.4 employees in twenty-five countries.

I've had the privilege of working with many alums of World Vision over the years. I've interviewed former leadership. I've been blessed to work with World Vision directly on several occasions, advising them on programs like the 30 Hour Famine, Team World Vision, and digital fundraising.

World Vision's size today is difficult to comprehend, but what is not hard to understand is that recurring giving has been the primary driver of its growth in individual contributions over the years.

From the early days of World Vision, after its founding in 1950 by Bob Pierce, child sponsorship was the cornerstone of the organization's efforts. The organization grew explosively in the 1980s, mainly in response to a dire famine in Ethiopia and innovative fundraising strategies in major channels like television.

My former boss and mentor, Steve Woodworth, was at the center of that effort, along with several other key leaders, leading all of marketing. During his time at World Vision, the organization grew from approximately $40 million annually to over $130 million in just twelve years.

One thing that has stood out to me from hearing stories of World Vision over the years was the central focus on recurring giving in the form of child sponsorship.

Bill Kliewer, a key figure on the World Vision leadership team for many years, once told me how intensely focused they were on the sponsorship program. Sponsorship was the key.

Charity: Water and its Singular Focus

In 2016, the team at charity: water launched a monthly giving program called The Spring. Launched at a time when the meteoric growth of the relatively new charity had subsided, founder Scott Harrison and his team were frustrated with the cycle of starting over on January 1 every year. The idea was to create an ongoing revenue stream by focusing almost exclusively on recurring giving.

It worked. By 2020, the program had more than 80,000 active recurring donors.

I asked Brady Josephson, VP of Marketing & Growth at charity: water, about this. The organization has done a number of really smart things over the years to grow their program, but for Josephson, the most important thing was their singular focus on The Spring—"The biggest thing to me was from our CEO and Founder to the Executive team to the Senior Leadership on down, there was *so much* commitment and alignment to growing our subscription giving program."

Josephson continued. "This focus and growth came at the detriment of some other things, but the whole org was like '*Spring, spring, spring.*'"

He went on. "That's the single most important thing for any nonprofit to grow subscription giving. You can do all the tactics and check all the boxes, but if you don't have that level of buy-in and commitment throughout the org, your growth is limited and slower."

A Good Kind of Unbalanced?

In some ways, conventional thinking contradicts how these organizations have prioritized recurring giving at the expense of other strategies and efforts.

"Don't put all your eggs in one basket."

"Best to have a diversified approach."

These sayings are good, most of the time—and we have language for the opposite approach—Unbalanced. Narrow-minded. Myopic. Risky.

Yet, at least some of the most successful charities raising most of the money through recurring giving have prioritized sustainer giving for years, even decades.

These organizations could be accused of being narrow-minded, losing revenue in other areas, and missing out on single-gift donors. At the same time, being "unbalanced" and prioritizing recurring donors has paid off. Now, years down the line, they have substantial, resilient sustainer programs.

This does not mean these organizations do not have healthy fundraising programs in other areas—single-gift direct marketing, major gifts, events, grants, legacy giving, and so on. In fact, many of them have quite sophisticated efforts in one or more of these other areas, often funded by their recurring revenue programs. It's just that they've adopted a mindset that they lead with recurring most of the time.

My hypothesis is that there are three reasons for the success of these programs.

1. **Focus**—Instead of dividing attention and resources, these charities poured their best efforts into a focused effort.

2. **Donor Attention**—I think donors can sense when an organization has prioritized creating a community of sustaining donors—an inner core, so to speak—and they respond well to that.
3. **Frequency**—When recurring giving is prioritized, there are more chances for recruitment efforts to break through, leading to greater response.

More research is needed on sustainer-first fundraising, but this is the closest I think I'll ever get to recommending being unbalanced and narrow-minded!

TAKEAWAY: A sustainer-first approach sends a clear message that the core of individuals who care deeply about the cause partner with the organization on a consistent, ongoing basis. The organization prioritizes building this long-term snowball of stable, sustainable support that enables the mission.

In our next chapter, we'll examine another question that regularly comes up—whether to have a named program.

CHAPTER 16

Incentivizing Action

G**ETTING IN FRONT** of your audience with a message is just the beginning. Along the journey of moving from awareness to interest to belief to action, one way to help boost the final step of conversion is to incentivize the individual to act.

Incentives can play a role at every stage of the journey in acquiring and keeping recurring donors—from prospect acquisition to sustainer acquisition, donor conversion, sustainer cultivation, upgrading, retention, and reactivation.

> Incentives can play a role at every stage of the journey in acquiring and keeping recurring donors

This chapter will discuss the most common incentives used across strategies, including the pros and cons for each.

Incentives take different forms. In the consumer world, incentives are often value-oriented—a discounted initial price or bonus materials. In the world of sustainable fundraising, incentives are also value-oriented, but in a different way.

Let's look at the nine of the most common types of incentives organizations use to move donors into giving on a recurring basis.

- Matches and Challenge Grants
- Multipliers
- Bonus Materials
- Front-End Premiums
- Back-End Premiums
- Deadlines and Goals
- Benefits
- Bounce Backs
- Sweepstakes

Matches and Challenge Grants

Matches and challenge grants are strong incentives to increase conversion by increasing the perceived value and impact of the gift. Most commonly, a donor match is a gift by an individual or group of donors, typically large donors, who commit to match, dollar for dollar, the giving of any new recurring donors.

The match could be for the first gift, the first few months of recurring giving, or even the first full year.

Similar to matches, challenge grants also multiply the giving of new or existing donors who step up to give. But unlike a match, challenge grants don't require donations to be given to release the funds. There is some evidence that challenge grants are not as effective as matching grants.

Either such grant has been proven to be motivating to would-be donors, increasing giving and conversion.

The cons are more limited but include the need to solicit matching or challenge gifts, often from other donors (often major donors) or from the organization's board.

TAKEAWAY: Matching and challenge gifts are powerful ways to incentivize potential donors to start a recurring gift by extending the impact the donor can have on their giving.

Another type of incentive is a multiplier, which is closely related to a match.

Multipliers

A multiplier is when the impact of each dollar given will be multiplied, usually through the value of donated goods or services.

One common situation is for organizations that distribute donated goods such as medical supplies or food—these gifts in kind (GIK) donations have a monetary value. Because the charity does not need to purchase these goods, the dollars raised are only needed for things like distribution, administration, and the like. A one-dollar donation might result in ten dollars' or twenty dollars' worth of impact.

By pairing recurring cash donations with donated goods, each donor's gift is multiplied five times, ten times, twenty times, or more.

A less common but still powerful form of multiplier is the donation of services. For example, some nonprofits operate clinics with professionals who donate their services, or volunteers donate time to pack supplies or serve in other ways. Because the nonprofit does not need to pay for these services, and the services have value, the organization can calculate the value of the donated services, which can be used as a multiplier.

Consider the following scenario—a nonprofit organization operates a clinic that provides services to people in need. The clinic costs $100,000 a year to operate, between overhead, administration, facilities, utilities, and the like.

However, the clinic is staffed by volunteers and professionals who donate their time to provide services. The organization tracks these services rendered and values them at $900,000. So, for $100,000 in spending, the clinic delivers $1,000,000 in value. In this case, every dollar donated enables ten dollars in impact—a great deal for donors!

Consider that for your organization even if you don't take donated goods. Do you have professionals and volunteers who donate services to your organization? Could that be used as a multiplier incentive for donors?

TAKEAWAY: Multipliers are a great way to help donors feel the power of donated goods and services, stretching each donation multiple times.

Next, let's look at bonus materials.

Bonus Materials

Every organization has expertise, and often, that expertise can be packaged in a way that would be valuable to donors in the form of materials of value to donors.

Typically, these bonus materials are digitally oriented items that are given to those who become donors. These items might take the form of guides, e-books, audio programs, videos, curriculum, or any number of items that are of value to potential donors.

In the area of influencer and artist programs, sometimes the bonus material is related to the influencer offering something of value from them to the potential donor—a free music track, a behind-the-scenes piece of content, and so on.

TAKEAWAY: Bonus materials are items of value offered as an incentive in exchange for the donor's commitment to give monthly.

Let's discuss premiums next. Premiums are typically physical items—there are two types of premiums or gifts: front-end premiums and back-end premiums. Let's start by looking at front-end premiums.

Front-End Premiums

A front-end premium is provided to a donor before they commit to give. These are often used as gestures of goodwill, ways to grab potential donors' attention, and to create a feeling of reciprocity or even guilt in some cases. The idea is that "we've sent you this item of value," whether it's a calendar, a set of return labels, greeting cards, or notepads, and "we hope you will reciprocate."

Front-end premiums can feel manipulative, but they also can align with what your organization does. For example, if you help enable micro-enterprise to budding entrepreneurs, then offering some small symbol of what your micro-entrepreneurs create can be a great way of getting attention and invoking the reciprocity mentioned previously.

Let's now look at back-end premiums.

Back-End Premiums

A back-end premium is a reward provided based on the donor's decision to sign up. It is often exchanged for a minimum recurring donation. Done right, it can be a strong incentive to sign up and increase average recurring-gift value.

Back-end premiums can be books, identity-related items such as mugs, bumper stickers, art, tote bags, or any number of other things.

I would encourage you to think about what fits within your organization's brand, who you are, and who your recurring donors are. The closer the premium is to the identity of your cause and your recurring giving program, the more quality donors you will attract.

Consider what your donors are used to. Have you used premiums before? If you haven't, do you want to start now?

TAKEAWAY: Premiums can help incentivize conversion to recurring giving. Front-end premiums are given before a donation is made, creating reciprocity and engagement to facilitate conversion. Back-end premiums incentivize action by offering something extra that aligns with the organization's cause and values.

The next type of approach that incentivizes action are deadlines and goals.

Deadlines and Goals

A good deadline creates a sense of urgency and helps to answer the question "Why now?" If the organization has done a good job of inspiring the would-be donor to understand the "Why," a deadline answers the question, "Why now?"

Ideally, the deadline is grounded in some reality that would be understandable to donors. "We are looking for one hundred donors to step up to give monthly by June 1, *so that* we can launch the new summer program with confidence" has more power than "We want you to act by June 1" with no explanation of why.

Similarly, goals create specificity around the action we want donors to take, giving a sense of the need's scope. When we say we are looking for "eighty-five more donors to stand with us," potential donors can imagine themselves being one of those eighty-five donors. People like to accomplish goals, especially toward the end when a goal is nearly accomplished.

TAKEAWAY: Deadlines create a sense of urgency, and goals create a sense of specificity and impact that can help move people to action.

Let's look at the next type of incentive in recurring giving programs—benefits.

Benefits

Benefits are often associated with membership programs and involve some form of value that the sustainer receives for participating in the program.

Benefits are common in membership-based programs and can include things such as discounts, exclusive or early access, personalized care, publications, events, resources, or special features.

TAKEAWAY: Benefits are designed to provide added value to donors, encouraging loyalty and ongoing engagement with the organization.

Next, let's look at a common strategy for incentivizing action—using bounce-back devices.

Bounce Backs

In direct marketing, bounce backs are a close cousin to front-end premiums. They are items of value sent to donors in advance of a gift. But rather than the item being for the donor, the idea is for the donor to interact with and return the item to the charity, often to be distributed to beneficiaries.

A classic example of a bounce-back is a birthday card for a sponsored child. The charity sends a physical greeting to the donor, encouraging them to write a note to their sponsored child, perhaps including a photo or something made by the donor's children, and make a donation to help celebrate the child and support the program.

In this way, the premium is "bounced back" to the charity for distribution, providing something of value to the program and a donation from the donor to support the work.

Bounce backs can also be used to acquire a new recurring donor, as an involvement device and a way to encourage the would-be donor to participate in the charity's work.

TAKEAWAY: Bounce backs are devices that donors are encouraged to return to the charity, creating an opportunity for involvement between the donor and charity, and incentivizing action.

The last and generally least common tactic in recurring gift fundraising is the use of sweepstakes, raffles, or games.

Sweepstakes, Raffles, Games

According to Double the Donation, a software platform that enables matching gifts, 47 percent of donors support nonprofit causes through online raffles or sweepstakes. This makes it surprising that so few charities participate in sweepstakes. The essence is that the donor receives a prize or prizes in exchange for a donation.

Both sweepstakes and raffles work by giving donors a chance to win a prize or prizes in exchange for a donation. Raffles are not allowed in every state since regulators consider raffles to be a form of gambling since donors pay in exchange for a chance to win something. At the same time, sweepstakes are more limited because they must include a free method of entry in addition to donation-based entries.

This is not meant to be an exhaustive examination of the role of sweepstakes in recurring giving and certainly is not legal advice—check with your legal expert before offering such a program. However, it is increasingly evident that some donors are responsive to the idea of a donation leading to a potential prize.

TAKEAWAY: In some cases, fundraising raffles and charity sweepstakes offer an attractive potential strategy to raise funds online. Raffles may not be allowed depending on your geographic location and local laws. In this case, a fundraising sweepstakes may be a good idea. Still, organizations need to consider legal implications and choose a provider that supports sweepstakes' official rules and a free method of entry without the need for a donation.

> Incentives can play a positive role at every stage in the journey of a recurring donor.

There are many ways to incentivize would-be and existing donors to take a next step. These incentives can play a positive role at every stage in the journey of a recurring donor.

In our next and final chapter for part 2 of this book, we'll step back and explore a big question—what is the purpose of a nonprofit?

CHAPTER 17
The Purpose of a Nonprofit

The purpose of business is to create and keep a customer.
—Peter Drucker

FAMED BUSINESS EDUCATOR, author, and consultant Peter Drucker—considered the father of modern management theory—is famous for saying that the purpose of a business is to create and keep customers. Three things strike me about this statement.

First, its simplicity. At the end of the day, business exists to create customers and serve them so that they remain customers.

Second, the emphasis on the second half of the phrase—"*and keep a customer.*" Business, when it's at its best and most healthy, has always balanced the acquisition of customers with retention of them. It's more expensive to find new customers. It's more profitable to keep them.

Third, it causes me to consider whether the purpose of a nonprofit is to create and keep a donor. What if a core role, maybe even *the* core role, of a charity is to incite passion in the hearts and minds of individuals to care about a cause and then step up to do something about it?

Subscriptions play a key role in keeping customers. They are designed on purpose to provide such a valuable ongoing service that customers stay with them month after month, year after year.

What if the purpose of a nonprofit was to create and keep a donor?

Dan Pallotta, entrepreneur, author, and humanitarian activist, is the author of *Uncharitable—How Restraints on Nonprofits Undermine Their Potential.* In the book, Pallotta challenges historical limitations placed on nonprofit organizations and exhorts us all to think differently about the role and scale of charity in the role today.[34]

Pallotta gave a now-famous TED Talk several years ago titled "The Way We Think about Charity Is Dead Wrong." As of writing, that talk has over 6.5 million views. In the talk, he makes a statement that is simple, but powerful.

> Philanthropy is the market for love.
>
> —Dan Pallotta

Think about that for a moment. *Philanthropy is the market for love.*

His point is that business and the market economy work very well for the 85 percent of people who can take advantage of them, but in any developed economy, there are always people who are left out, and there are intractable problems that businesses can't or won't solve—that's where nonprofits come in.

I take Pallotta's point as a challenge to the nonprofit sector. We are marketing a "product" as charities, and that product is love.

You may cringe at the idea of *marketing love.* I know I did at first. Am I saying that charities are hawking love? Is our job to be marketers for love? Doesn't that diminish the very essence of love?

In an interview on *We Are for Good*, a podcast hosted by Jon McCoy and Becky Endicott to help nonprofit organizations be more effective in their work, Pallotta expanded on philanthropy as the market for love.

> And so this is why I said in the TED Talk that philanthropy is the market for love. And I meant that seriously, not as like a Hallmark card. *It's the market for all those people for whom there is no other market coming.* Because you can monetize love. People want to feel love. People want to give love. They're willing to pay for that, in the same way they want to taste chocolate. In the same way they want to listen to music and other ephemeral experiences. We just need to excite demand for love at that level by unleashing the nonprofit sector, unleashing its voice, giving it voice the same way Coca Cola has voice, giving it capital so that it can amplify that voice the same way Apple is able to amplify that voice and create a country, a community a world of compassion, as much as consumption.
>
> —Dan Pallotta

Philanthropy is the market for love.

I remember the day I learned in business school that Nike is not a shoe company. It's not even a "lifestyle brand" (whatever that means). No, Nike is a marketing company. Nike exists to create the market for optimum athletic performance. Sure, part of executing on that vision is designing and manufacturing a product. But their core purpose is to create demand for optimum athletic performance.

Like Nike, nonprofits like the Humane Society of the United States, charity: water, World Vision, St. Jude—and I hope your charity—are participating in creating the market of love.

TAKEAWAY: Subscription companies are "in the business of creating and keeping customers," as Peter Drucker suggested many years ago. If charities are the market for love, what if charity leaders saw their role as creating and keeping donors?

The Purpose of a Nonprofit—To Create and Keep Donors

In the next section of this book, we'll get into the process of building and sustaining a thriving recurring giving program.

As we do, I want you to consider the purpose of a charity. Whether you are a nonprofit fundraiser, a donor, or someone passionate about the philanthropic sector—or all three—I want to challenge you.

> What if you saw your role as helping people to participate in the market for love?

What if your purpose, as a leader and as an organization, was to create and keep donors? What if you saw your role as helping people to participate in the market for love? How might sustainable subscription giving enable you to accomplish that mission?

PART 3

Designing and Managing a Thriving Sustainer Program

CHAPTER 18

A Guide to a Thriving Sustainer Program

"**IF I WERE** in your shoes."

I've written this book as if I were in your shoes. If it were my responsibility, how would I design and grow your subscription giving program?

The only problem with putting myself in your shoes is that I don't know you or your context.

There are many potential next steps. So, I've outlined a seven-part guide to growing your recurring giving program. This guide is a soup-to-nuts summary of everything you need to know to create and manage a thriving sustainer program.

In this guide and throughout part 3, we'll cover the essential elements of a stable, growing, recurring giving program:

- Structure and Team
- Measurement
- Program Design

- Systems and Platforms
- Acquisition
- Conversion
- Cultivation
- Upgrading
- Retention
- Reactivation

Before I share the steps, I want to give you a tool you can use to diagnose and prioritize what to focus on next in your situation. This tool is something I've used throughout my career to prioritize next steps.

It's called the impact-effort matrix.[35]

Prioritizing Next Steps—The Impact-Effort Matrix

The most effective leaders recognize that everything cannot be a priority at the same time. As I've observed these leaders, one thing I've noticed is that they are extremely disciplined about focusing on one or, at most, a couple of things at the same time.

The most effective leaders recognize that everything cannot be a priority at the same time.

The impact-effort matrix is a tool for prioritizing efforts. It has roots in management and decision sciences and is easy to use to prioritize activities among many different options quickly.

I first learned about this tool from Steve Woodworth, CEO of Masterworks, when I served with him as executive vice president of Strategic Innovation. Steve had learned the tool during a stint as a senior consultant in a process re-engineering firm.

You can do this process in just a few minutes if you have a list of what you are trying to prioritize. Let's say you are considering ten different strategies or tactics. Write them out quickly, and rank them twice on a scale of one to ten, from lowest to highest:

Impact—what is the likely impact?

Effort—how much effort is likely required?

The first one to ten score, "Impact," is about how significant an impact you think the particular task or strategy would have on your program. A rating of one is the lowest, with almost no positive impact, and a ten is the highest impact.

The second one to ten score, "Effort," is about how much it will take to implement (resources, time, personnel, technology, etc.). Low effort would be a one—it's easy—I can do it right away. A ten requires significant effort—it's a heavy lift, even if it might have a high impact.

Once you've made your list, what you do is simply plot out these strategies and tactics on a quadrant like this:

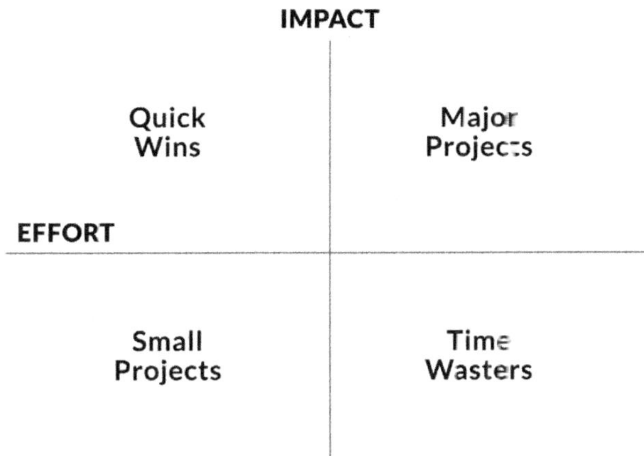

By plotting out potential strategies and tactics, you can see which efforts are likely to be quick wins , major projects, incremental small projects, and time wasters.

Items in the top left of the quadrant—those with low effort and high impact—are called "Quick Wins." Start there.

In the next quadrant on the upper right are areas with high impact but require high effort. These are "Major Projects"—you should only have things here that you believe will create an exponential impact because you will put a lot of effort into them.

The bottom half of this matrix is dangerous. It's where you have low-impact activities. The bottom-left is low effort but also low impact, and I recommend not spending much time here. This can be a dangerous space because it's easy to fill your plate with things that are busy work. Maybe they're easy to do, but they won't have much impact. We call this quadrant "Small Projects." Sure, there are likely to be a few easy things to knock out, but I highly recommend starting with the Quick Wins in the upper-left quadrant—they are also easy to do and likely have a higher impact.

The bottom-right quadrant—low impact, high effort—is the quadrant to avoid. These are "Time Wasters"—low impact and high effort. You might be surprised at how many organizations identify multiple time wasters in their programs when they look at things from this perspective. You have too much on your plate to spend time and effort doing things that will take a lot of effort but ultimately have low impact.

TAKEAWAY: Anytime you need to prioritize and have many things going on, I highly recommend using the impact-effort matrix to visualize what you have on your plate or what you are considering adding to your plate very quickly. This simple exercise will give you a new perspective on what to prioritize.

To recap the impact-effort matrix process:

- **Step 1—List Solutions:** Gather the potential activities you are considering focusing on next.
- **Step 2—Assess Solutions:** Quickly rate each activity twice, on a scale of one to ten—Impact and then Effort.
- **Step 3—Plot Solutions:** Place each solution in the appropriate quadrant based on your assessment.
- **Step 4—Prioritize:** Focus on the top half of the matrix, prioritizing *Quick Wins* that yield the highest return for the lowest effort and *Major Projects* that promise exponential results. Ignore the *Time Wasters* and strategically choose *Small Projects* with incremental results.

IMPACT-EFFORT MATRIX

IMPACT

EFFORT

Quick Wins	Major Projects
Small Projects	Time Wasters

Now that you have this tool to help you prioritize the activities you select to build your program, let me share a brief overview of what we'll cover in the coming chapters.

Steps to Designing and Growing a Thriving Sustainer Program

The remainder of part 3 of the book will walk you through a seven-step process to designing and growing a thriving sustainer program.

Let's briefly outline the steps here.

The remainder of part 3 of the book will walk you through a seven-step process to designing and growing a thriving sustainer program.

Step 1. Benchmark Where You Are

To know where you are going, you must know where you've been. Every organization is at a different stage and structure in the development of recurring giving programs. Understanding your stage of maturity and key measures can help you structure your program for success.

We'll cover this in:

Chapter 19: Identify Your Stage of Maturity—Structuring for Success

Chapter 20: Understand Where You Are—Measurement

Step 2. Understand Your Donors

The next step to designing and growing a thriving sustainer program is to put yourself in your donor's shoes, walk the journey, and identify the key moments to cultivate. This includes talking to donors and understanding what inspires them and how they experience the cause.

We'll cover this in:

Chapter 21: Go on Your Donor's Journey—Mapping the Experience
Chapter 22: Talk to Donors—Human-Centered Design

Step 3. Craft an Ongoing Value Proposition and Clear Offer

The subscription economy has made it critical to have a value proposition that justifies ongoing giving. The strength of your value proposition must exceed the friction of taking action. Consideration should also be given to the essentials of a strong and clear offer.

We'll cover this in:

Chapter 23: Craft an Ongoing Value Proposition—Connection with Need
Chapter 24: Develop Your Offer—Nailing the Essentials

Step 4. Get Your Technology Right

The technology that supports your sustainer efforts will be the single biggest barrier or opportunity to your program's growth. We'll discuss the subscription giving tech stack that undergirds strong recurring giving programs.

We'll cover this in:

Chapter 25: Get Your Tech Stack Right—Systems and Platforms

Step 5. Design Your Program

A subscription-ready recurring giving program includes a high-quality ongoing value proposition, clear identity, benefits for being involved, dedicated website presence, great onboarding experience, and ongoing cultivation.

We'll cover this in:

Chapter 26: Design and Launch (or Relaunch)—Program Design

Step 6. Grow Your Program

There are two primary ways to grow a sustainer program—acquire new donors who give a recurring gift right away or convert existing donors to recurring giving. We'll look at each of these and the channels and strategies that work best for each.

We'll cover this in:

Chapter 27: Grow Your Program—Recruit Everywhere

Step 7. Cultivate a Healthy Program

The true value of a recurring donor is that they become loyal, long-term supporters. Treat sustainers like the faithful core supporters they are. This includes how you onboard them, cultivate them on an ongoing basis, give them opportunities to upgrade their giving, retain them, and invite them to reactivate their giving if they lapse.

We'll cover this in:

Chapter 28: Cultivate a Healthy Program—Onboarding to Reactivation

We'll take each step in turn, but remember, this isn't meant to be implemented blindly. As you go, I would encourage you to list the tactics and strategies you think make sense for your stage in development and run them through the impact-effort matrix exercise outlined in the last section.

Finally, let me share a self-assessment tool we've developed to help you identify where you are and what you need to focus on next.

Sustainable Giving Growth Self-Assessment

We've developed a sustainable giving growth self-assessment that includes twenty questions and takes just ten minutes to complete.

You can take the assessment at www.imago.consulting/assessment.

After completing the assessment, you'll receive a personalized report on the next steps you should take to grow your recurring giving program.

Let's start growing our sustainer programs by evaluating our current stage of development and what to do next in light of where we are.

CHAPTER 19

Identify Your Stage of Maturity—Structuring for Success

THE FIRST STEP in building and managing a thriving sustainer program is to identify where you are. Every organization is at a different stage and structure in the development of recurring giving programs. Understanding your stage can help you structure your program for success.

There are four stages of maturity for sustainer programs:

- **Starter**—Just getting going.
- **Basic**—Some pieces are in place, possibly even a named program.
- **Intermediate**—Regular recruitment and cultivation.
- **Advanced**—Recurring is a centerpiece of fundraising and generates significant revenue.

Regardless of your stage, the most important principle in your program we discussed in chapter 12, and that is to make sure you have clear ownership.

No matter how you structure your program within your organization, one person should feel responsible for your sustainer program's overall care, feeding, and growth.

A friend of mine put it this way: "Who is sleeping on the cot?" In other words, who feels the pressure to ensure that the program is working well, that donors are taken care of, and that it's growing?

The one-word focus for structuring your organization for success at every stage is *responsibility.*

TAKEAWAY: The one-word focus for structuring your organization for success at every stage is *responsibility.* While you may have multiple team members engaged with the program, one person should feel responsible for its overall success.

Let's now examine how structure and resourcing differ at different stages of growth in a subscription giving program.

Resourcing at Different Stages of Maturity

Each organization is at a different place with regard to resourcing availability and the stage of maturity of the recurring giving program. Let's walk through the four core stages of growth, describing each stage and how you might think about structuring the program internally at your organization.

Starter Stage: Just Getting Going

The first stage of maturity includes organizations just starting with a recurring giving program.

Your organization might have had donors giving on a recurring basis for quite some time, but this is different from having a dedicated or mature program. I know organizations that have thousands of recurring donors that would still be in the starter stage.

Organizations in the starter stage have little beyond a checkbox or option for monthly giving on the website. Typically, no one person is responsible for recurring giving in stage one organizations.

Basic Stage: Investing in Growth

Organizations in the second stage have some efforts focused on growing the sustainer program. They may even have a named program.

Once the organization commits to growing the program and develops a plan to do so, one of the most important things an organization can do is ensure that one person is responsible for the success of the program.

For smaller organizations early on, the ideal person responsible will likely be the executive director or person in charge of development or marketing—or even a board member for management-oriented boards. Either way, it is likely to be a partial responsibility, with that individual responsible for other things within the organization.

The person responsible should have goals related to revenue, the number of recurring donors, retention, and long-term value, which we'll discuss in the next chapter.

For the advocate at this stage, this is often a partial responsibility. The size of the program may not justify a full-time person, but this person should have full responsibility.

The goal at this stage is that someone spends at least 60 percent of their time on the program, even if it's not initially. Something happens when a person spends the majority of their time focused on and feeling accountable for a thing's growth, which helps it grow.

Stage three, after the investing stage, is typically where the most rapid and significant growth occurs.

Intermediate Stage: Growing

In stage three, a program is up and running and typically sees significant returns for the organization. Still, in some ways, it is just getting started at creating a mature, thriving program.

At this stage, you're going to want to look at having a dedicated lead, somebody responsible for the program overall. This does not mean they do everything themselves. Often, they work with other departments and other personnel to grow the program. Still, this person is more or less dedicated full-time to leading the work within the organization.

The most significant difference between stage two and stage three organizations is that increasingly dedicated resources are allocated in stage three. There may be some full-time individuals focused on the effort, but more likely, there is a growing number of individuals for whom the sustainer program is a significant priority.

The fourth stage of maturity is a thriving subscription giving program.

Advanced: Thriving

In stage four, we move from a dedicated lead to a dedicated team. These personnel specialize in and spend the majority of their time growing and cultivating a thriving, recurring giving program.

It might start with a producer or a project manager role or analyst, but it can extend into creative and production resources as the program grows.

Again, at every stage along this journey, it is important that one individual feels responsible for the program. If everyone is responsible, then no one is responsible.

TAKEAWAY: The structure of your team and responsibilities will shift as you move from just starting to investing in growth, growing, and operating a thriving program. At each step along the way, there should always be someone who feels the responsibility and accountability for the program's success.

Lastly, as you think about structuring for success, it's important to remember that your team is not just those on the payroll.

Building Your Team by Leveraging Outside Resources

Most nonprofits have far too much work to do compared to the amount of paid staff to handle it. It isn't just about your own internal staff resources but also about building your team by leveraging outside resources.

At every stage of maturity, consider your broader network of people, platforms, and expertise as you build your team. Not everyone on your team needs to be a staff member.

There are many ways to build your team with limited dedicated staff resources. These can include the following:

- Contractors
- Agencies

- Consultants
- Volunteers
- Technology, Tools, and Platforms

Every one of these resources can play a role in making your program thrive. The benefits of leveraging outside resources go well beyond just the limited time that your staff has.

Benefits of using outside partners and tools include:

Expertise—When utilizing outside resources, you can be much narrower about identifying and using the right expertise. Individuals and firms specializing in recurring giving can help avoid many pitfalls and common mistakes and help you put the right effort into the right areas.

Cost—Using contractors or other outside resources, you can spin up or down expenditures much more quickly and often. You can buy expertise that you might not be able to afford in a full-time employee. While that outside contractor or consultant may seem expensive, they're a lot cheaper than if you were to hire somebody with equivalent expertise and capability.

Flexibility—Besides managing costs, you can bring in outside resources as needed, "just in time." You don't need somebody on your payroll all of the time for a specific season of the year in which you might need to take the next step or build out a project. If you need a major push to develop a new set of assets, for example, having partners you can call on is a powerful way of getting a bunch of work done.

Quality—Another benefit of leveraging outside resources is quality, which is related to expertise from the previous point. When you pay outsiders to do work, their ability to continue to do good work is based on their ability to bring good quality. Partners who specialize in these types of work undoubtedly already have processes, systems, tools, training, and personnel that will result in a quality product that would take longer or be impossible using internal resources.

Timing/Resource Allocation—The last area to consider when you think about building your team outside of internal staff, in addition to internal staff, is timing and resource allocation. You get what you need when you need it. The last thing to consider with outside resources is your ability to allocate them when you need them. When you are working on your program, some skills are critical but not needed all of the time, so it doesn't justify having somebody on staff in a full-time capacity when you only need that expertise or skill set at one point. And as I mentioned earlier, hiring in the first place may be cost-prohibitive.

TAKEAWAY: Consider how you build your team, not just with internal or staff resources, but through the network of individuals, platforms, and tools you have at your disposal.

One final note as we consider structuring for success—growing subscription giving requires an investment mentality.

Growing Subscription Giving Requires Investment

It's not uncommon for for-profit subscription-based companies to take several years to reach profitability. They are patient and understand the rewards in the form of profitability and huge returns that come as they scale the program.

The nature of recurring giving is a lot like compounding interest—in the early days, it might be modest, but over time, it is a snowball that gains momentum.

As you think about what stage you're in developing your recurring program, consider over-investing relative to where you are today. The benefits of compounding are well worth the investment.

Amy Konary from the Subscribed Institute shares, “You are going to want to have likely a dedicated team, and that dedicated team should be a team that really understands that segment really well. Thinking about it as a start-up within your own business and really take the principles of customer centricity and future proofing to heart.”

TAKEAWAY: Adopt an investment mindset, understanding the rewards from compounding returns that accumulate pay dividends for years to come.

Next, we’ll look at one of the most essential elements of cultivating a successful program—measurement.

CHAPTER 20

Understand Where You Are—Measurement

TO KNOW WHERE you are going, you must know where you've been. We'll cover the four core metrics that every nonprofit leader should measure and more advanced metrics and key reports to review.

Bobb Biehl, who I've quoted elsewhere in this book, has a saying—"Nothing clarifies like measurability. Nothing motivates like results." If you know where you want to go and how much progress you are making along the way, that direction and clarity creates momentum.

Put another way, how can you know where you are going if you don't know where you've been?

If nothing clarifies like measurability, most nonprofits don't have a grasp on the state of their recurring revenue programs.

Don't be like those nonprofits that have no clue where their program is at or where it is going. This is a critical program for sustainably fueling charity and deserves to be measured.

As with any fundraising or marketing program, the sheer number of things you can measure are overwhelming. Let's look at what you should measure first.

Four Core Metrics

For organizations at all maturity levels, four core metrics should be understood and tracked on an ongoing basis.

We'll start with these four metrics before going on to any more advanced measurements:

1. Total active recurring donors
2. Total revenue from recurring donors (all sources)
3. Percentage of total revenue from recurring donors
4. Long-term value (LTV) of recurring donors

Let's look at each core four metrics and define them:

1. Number of Active Recurring Donors—The number of subscription donors who have given a recurring gift in the past year. This reflects the size of your active sustainer file.

2. Total Revenue from Recurring Donors (All Sources)—The total giving from recurring donors, including all recurring and nonrecurring gifts. Express this total revenue in monthly and annual terms, known as MRR and ARR, respectively—monthly recurring revenue and annual recurring revenue.

Bonus points if you break down revenue from recurring gifts versus nonrecurring gifts. Recurring donors make some of the best one-time givers. It is common to see 25 percent or more of giving from recurring donors in nonrecurring gift revenue.

3. Percentage of Total Revenue from Recurring Donors—Divide your total revenue from recurring donors by total organization revenue to determine the percentage of your current revenue from recurring donors. This percentage of organization revenue can vary widely depending on the type and maturity of your sustainer program. Many one-to-one sponsorship and membership programs see 80-plus percent of their revenue from recurring gifts. However, for most recurring giving programs, it's more common to see 10–25 percent of contributions from recurring donors. If you are at 10 percent or below, consider the opportunities for growth. From 10 to 25 percent, you are likely in the basic or intermediate stage of maturity. At 25 percent–plus for nonsponsorship and nonmembership giving is pretty good—consider how to add fuel to the fire.

4. Long-Term Value (LTV) of Recurring Donors—Total giving per recurring donor over sixty months (five years). By definition, you won't know this precisely until a donor has reached the five-year mark after signing up for recurring giving. With this data, you can estimate and project the LTV of new sustainers based on history. Long-term value is the most important metric to track, so it's worth the work to come to a reasonable estimate of your five-year LTV for recurring donors.

If you need to estimate LTV, my friend Jon Van Wyk recommends creating a sustainer LTV factor. Jon is one of the best strategic analysts I've ever worked with and has worked with many sustainer programs over the years. He has found that if you take your five-year LTV estimate and divide it by your average recurring gift, you can create a factor. For example, for one client that factor is 35. For another, it is 45. When you have this, you can take any new recurring donor and estimate their LTV. For example, with a factor of 45, a new $37/month donor will have an estimated LTV of $1,665 (factor of 45 times $37 average recurring gift = $1,665 estimated LTV). If you are just getting started and have no idea, 35 times average gift is a good starting point.

There are many possible metrics to track. It is vital that you track the progress of your program via these four core metrics—active sustainers, total revenue, percentage of total, and LTV. You can then add more advanced metrics as you get into the rhythm.

A Note on Measuring Outcomes versus Inputs

One of the mistakes I see charities make is an overreliance on measuring only the *outcomes* or *end results* of what they are doing. The problem with only measuring outcomes is that it can take time for results to show. Particularly with sustainer giving and the power of long-term value, more than measuring only outcomes is required.

> There are two kinds of things we can measure—outcomes and inputs. The key is that the *inputs* should lead to the *outcomes.*

There are two kinds of things we can measure—outcomes and inputs. Outcomes are those measurable things that give us a read on how things are working. But we can also measure inputs—things we can measure along the way to creating outcomes. Inputs can be activities such as number of emails, campaigns, and so on. Or they can be non-donation-related engagement—clicks, views, traffic, new names, participation, and so on. The key is that the *inputs* should lead to the *outcomes.*

We'll start with critical outcomes to measure, but every organization should also seek to understand the inputs that lead to those outcomes.

Intermediate Stage Sustainer Metrics

If you are ready for the next level of maturity, the following metrics will help you see where you can improve the program:

5. Average Recurring Gift—The average recurring gift amount from recurring donors is a helpful short-term guide for the value of the current sustainers in your program. Note that if you have a lot of sustainers that give significant gifts (e.g., $100–$500+), it is helpful to look at the median recurring gift to see what level the majority of your sustainers are giving.

6. Number of New and Converted Recurring Donors—The only way the program grows is by adding more sustainers than those you lose each year. Track the number of newly acquired donors who are sustainers and the number of existing donors who convert to recurring donors.

7. Churn (Retention) of Recurring Donors—Most nonprofits express the loss of recurring donors in a program in terms of retention—as in, "We retained 85 percent of our recurring donors from last year to this." A more impactful alternative would be to express the churn in terms of the percentage of donors who did not give again from last year to this (e.g., "We had a churn rate of 15 percent."). I prefer churn—candidly, it's more painful and motivating to hear "We're losing 15 percent of our donors" than "We're retaining 85 percent of our donors."

8. Reactivation of Recurring Donors—The number of sustainers who stopped giving that have since reactivated this year. These metrics will show you how well you are doing with renewing former recurring donors.

9. Cost to Acquire a Recurring Donor—The average cost to acquire a new recurring donor. This typically is based on the cost of paid media, not including soft costs such as staff time, since most organizations don't track soft costs in a way conducive to measurement.

Advanced-Stage Sustainer Metrics

More advanced sustainer programs add a few more key metrics.

10. Net Payback Period—Time (in months) to break even on the acquisition cost minus any one-time gifts. This is a powerful concept that I first heard about in the nonprofit sector from Brady Josephson. Drawn from similar metrics used in subscription businesses, I've seen multiple nonprofits use this metric.

The idea is to estimate how long it takes to make back the acquisition cost. Often, sustainer recruitment efforts result in single gifts, and we know the value of a recurring donor is in their subsequent giving, so this approach accounts for both. The basic formula is:

> (Total Spend – Revenue from Single Gifts)/(New Recurring Donors × Average Recurring Gift) = Net Payback Period

Using this math, you might see a net payback of thirteen months or eighteen months. I've seen as low as two to four months net payback, though that is hard to maintain at scale.

11. Recurring Giving by Payment Type and Channel—Knowing that the highest retaining payment type is EFT, organizations break down the number of recurring gifts, average gifts, revenue, and LTV by payment type—typically looking at EFT, Credit Card, and Other Methods. Likewise, the channel in which the sustainer is acquired strongly influences performance and donor value.

By monitoring the mix of payment types and channels, the organization can better predict churn and focus on efforts to convert donors to more stable payment types.

12. Net Cost Per New Recurring Donor—A combination of net payback period and cost to acquire a recurring donor, this composite metric accounts for income from campaigns to offset the cost of acquisition.

(Spend – One-Time Revenue)/(New Recurring Donors)
= Net Cost Per New Recurring Donor

This is a little more advanced version of the cost per donor, but it is more strategic because it recognizes that one-time donations offset the cost of acquisition, bringing down the cost per new recurring donor.

TAKEAWAY: The outcomes of a healthy sustainer program consist of the number of recurring donors, revenue, average gift, percentage of total, and long-term value. As programs mature, additional metrics are helpful to dial in and truly grow the program.

Let's wrap up this chapter by considering key reports to review and how often.

Key Reports to Review

There are three kinds of reports that should be utilized to manage and grow a sustainer program:

- Sustainer dashboard
- Campaign reports
- Channel reports

The Sustainer Dashboard measures the health of the sustainer file and should be reviewed at least quarterly, possibly monthly if you have it set up well. This dashboard is the main place for the metrics outlined earlier in this chapter and provides a view of the file's health at a glance. It is the first place you should detect issues, such as increased churn or a drop in the number of new sustainers.

Campaign Reports are focused reviews of your major initiatives in your sustainer program. These might be micro campaigns or reactivation campaigns. A campaign report is essentially a roll-up of the next type of report we'll discuss—the channel report. A campaign report helps answer the question, "How did the campaign do versus our objectives?" These reports should be reviewed after every campaign or initiative.

Channel Reports are detailed breakdowns of performance by channel. This is the most likely place where you can review both inputs (activity, engagement) and outcomes (results) and discern what is working and what is not. Note that some channels are great at generating activity and engagement but are less likely to be attributed to outcomes, such as social media. This doesn't mean that social media is ineffective—it's just a recognition that some channels generate demand, and others are where donors choose to act. Channel reports should be reviewed monthly at a minimum, though depending on the nature of the team and the size of the operation, they may be reviewed weekly or even daily.

TAKEAWAY: Reports are the main way charity leaders can uncover what is working, what is not, what to change, and what to double down on. A dashboard indicates the health of the sustainer file, while campaign and channel reports are deeper dives into the mechanics of what strategies and tactics are doing.

Let's now look at the donor journey holistically and the practice of cultivating powerful moments.

CHAPTER 21

Go On Your Donor's Journey—Mapping the Experience

YOUR DONORS ARE going on a journey with your organization, whether you recognize it or not. This journey shapes the experience that donors have with your brand.

It is common for the donor journey to consist of a collection of disconnected experiences—communications from different teams or interactions with different departments.

It's important to be intentional with your donor journey. There are three steps to understanding your donor journey and infusing it with powerful moments:

1. Map the Existing Journey
2. Understand Reality
3. Identify the Key Moments

Donor journeys can devolve into a collection of disconnected experiences.

The first step to cultivating an intentional journey for recurring donors is to map it out as it exists today.

Step One: Mapping the Existing Journey

First, capture everything you believe you know about the existing donor journey. What are all the communications and touch points from the beginning of the relationship to no longer giving to the organization?

Consider all potential inbound, outbound, and passive touch points with your organization.

Inbound touch points include anything where the donor initiates or interacts with the organization. These might include donor services, the website, the donation process, the physical location, the volunteer program, and so on.

Outbound touch points are those you might typically think of as our donor experience—things you send to donors, including communications such as email, paid digital media, phone, direct mail, and so on.

Passive touch points are those elements in which donors experience you without acting—your content, organic (unpaid) social media, collateral, and so on.

Map out each of these items by life stage. Typical life stages are (1) before they are a donor, (2) once they are a donor, and (3) after they are no longer a donor.

TAKEAWAY: Based on everything you know about the donor experience, create a map of the existing journey for donors. This will give you an overview of what you believe the donor journey to be, which will come in handy in the next step when you seek to understand reality.

The next step is understanding reality because it most likely differs from what you think it is.

Step Two: Understand Reality

The truth is that the donors' experiences are never quite what we think they are. I've worked on dozens of donor journeys over the years, and I can't think of a single time when the experience was precisely what the organization thought it was.

The difference between what we *think* our donor journey is, and what it *actually* is, is due to various factors. Systems change over time, processes break, donors interact in ways we haven't planned, and data practices can greatly impact the donor experience.

Secret Donor Study

At Imago Consulting, we conduct an evaluation of every organization we work with. We essentially enter the organization through various entry points and document the entire experience, from searching for the organization to signing up or giving a gift to canceling. Every journey we've mapped has resulted in major insights into the donor experience and how to improve it.

Every journey we've mapped has resulted in major insights into the donor experience and how to improve it.

Many of the realizations in a secret donor study are what I call "facepalm moments," because the insights are so obvious in hindsight. But this is why mapping the donor experience is so important.

You can do this yourself, or you can have a third party like Imago Consulting do it. There are advantages to having an outside group do the study—objectivity, perspective, and experience with other donor journeys. Also, outsiders are less likely to justify why things are how they are, which is common when inside staff or stakeholders are mapping the journey.

TAKEAWAY: Seek to understand reality by having someone experience the donor journey firsthand through secret donor research. Identify those key moments that seem to be particularly remarkable highs or negative lows. This will prepare you for the final step—identifying the key moments to focus on.

Step Three: Identify the Key Moments

Once you understand the reality of your donor journey, the best thing you can do is cultivate powerful moments.

Once you understand the reality of your donor journey, the best thing you can do is cultivate powerful moments. In *The Power of Moments,* Dan and Chip Heath argue that humans tend to misunderstand how our memories work.

We tend to think that our memories are the average of all our experiences with a brand.

For example, consider a trip to Disneyland. You might be tempted to think that your Disney experience is basically the average of the highs, lows, and midpoints coming together to make some sort of cohesive memory, good or bad, of your trip. But that's different from how brain scientists and psychologists have learned how our memories work.

When reviewing your donor journey, your goal should be to *elevate the peaks* and *flip the pits.*

We are far more wired to remember what Dan and Chip Heath call the *peaks,* the *pits,* the *milestones,* and the *transitions.* In other words, certain powerful moments stand out in our memories far more than the average little pothole or moments we quickly forget. This is so important because when you map out and understand your recurring donor journey, you will identify a hundred things that could or should be better.

There are only a very small handful of powerful moments that donors remember, either because they're a pit and a poor experience for donors or, in a positive way, because they're a peak moment. When reviewing your donor journey, your goal should be to *elevate the peaks* and *flip the pits.*

Elevate the Peaks and Flip the Pits

Elevate the peaks means identifying our best moments and enhancing them even further. Many organizations miss the opportunity to highlight their donors' best moments when there is so much more they can do to accentuate those peaks.

I remember an organization that gave a peak moment to our family eight years ago, and we are still monthly givers to that organization today, even though we haven't had very many experiences with it since then. It was such a powerful moment that we continue to give.

Likewise, if you have a deep pit or a very negative experience, the question is first, "How can we flip that pit and turn it into a peak?" Not just, "How can we fill in the pothole and make it a little bit better?" But instead, "Can we truly reimagine that experience in a way that turns it from a liability in our donor experience into an asset at a peak moment?"

TAKEAWAY: Once you've identified the highest peaks and lowest pits, seek to elevate the peaks and flip the pits to create memorable moments that will stay with donors for the long run.

Next, let's look at the importance of talking to donors, both in program design and in identifying improvements to the program.

CHAPTER 22

Talk to Donors—Human-Centered Design

OUTSIDE OF DOCUMENTING the existing reality by mapping the donor journey, the next step is to talk to donors. Look for opportunities to speak to your recurring donors one-on-one. The goal is to gather insights and to stay close to the donor.

Why do they give? What was the experience that led them to be passionate about the cause in the first place? Talk to people who are donors and ask them about that experience.

Ask indirect questions that lead to insights like, "Tell me about the best experience you've ever had with giving." Listen and watch for those moments when their eyes light up or they are frustrated. Those are the signals for areas to pay attention to.

Having an outsider talk to donors can be a good idea—they will be less biased. It can also help donors give better feedback since donors tend to tell you what they think you want to hear or get stuck thinking they are providing professional advice to the nonprofit, not authentically reflecting on their own experience.

The Importance of Understanding Donor Motivation

In chapter 10, we featured Allen Thornburgh, principal and executive producer at Sublimity, a studio that helps leaders create, launch, and scale bold new experiences that their audiences love.

Thornburgh advocates for nonprofits to leverage human-centered design in order to move beyond guessing at what their prospective and current donors value by talking to them. He and his team seek to understand not only why donors give in their own words but, deeper than that, to understand what fires their imagination and ignites their passion, in addition to what kinds of giving experiences have left a lasting impression.

Thornburgh has seen that a key to designing a successful program that will resonate with the audience is truly understanding the donors and their underlying motivations.

> A key to designing a successful subscription giving program is truly understanding the donors and their underlying motivations.

These insights then become the seeds of inspiration as the team seeks to conceptualize and design a program, including its name, essence, brand, and ultimately, the full scope of the program—value proposition, offer, pricing, benefits, and presence.

Let's look at an example of how insights from talking to donors can shape a recurring giving program.

Case Study—Mission Aviation Fellowship's Flight Crew

The team at Sublimity worked with Mission Aviation Fellowship (MAF) to design and launch a recurring giving program. Using their approach to human-centered design, the team interviewed donors.

Many insights emerged from those interviews, one of which was very interesting, which came from an interview with a gentleman named Jace from Iowa (his name has been changed to protect his privacy).

Jace owned a farm and donated to Mission Aviation Fellowship. When the interviewer asked him about supporting charities involved with aviation, Allen shared, "That made him think about and articulate a game that he and his son play, where they hear a plane fly overhead and each guesses how many engines it has, what type of plane it is, and who the carrier is, and then whoever's more right has won the game."

Wanting to learn more, Allen asked him, "What do you do? Do you run outside and look up in the air? And he laughed and said, 'No, we've got this flight-tracker app, which he showed me.'"

It was a striking insight for Allen. "So with the remaining interviews, we kept asking people, do you use a flight-tracker app on your phone? And if so, what do you use it for? And nearly everybody we talked to had a flight-tracker app on their phone, or their spouse had a flight-tracker app. And every time they talked about what they do with it, they had some level of enthusiasm about this flight-tracker app as well. And whenever they described what they did with it, they lit up."

Among other things, the team identified something that fired the donors' imagination—the "aviation" part of Mission *Aviation* Fellowship.

As the team debriefed and began to dream about the program, this fascination with aviation was paired with another idea: Mission Aviation Fellowship "took the Gospel to the ends of the earth." There was something very exciting, special, and unique about the fact that

MAF was transporting resources, supplies, and people to the remotest places on earth.

These insights from talking to donors planted the seeds for the program that would eventually take shape. After a collaborative process with the MAF team, the winning concept was taken back to donors for validation. That concept was known as "Flight Crew," a monthly giving program to "reach people in the most isolated places with the love of Jesus."

The website describes Flight Crew, saying, "Flight Crew Members enable MAF to answer the call when every second counts. To fly into remote places when emergencies strike. To deliver hope at someone's most desperate moment. To save lives."

When the team launched the new program, they projected one-year goals. When they achieved their entire first-year goals in *just five weeks*, Allen knew they were on the right track.

While his team has refined this craft over the past several years, Thornburgh offers several tips on how to seek donor insights without resorting to generic surveys or "why do you give" questions.

- Don't just guess at what your donors value and ask them to validate your guesses. Instead, actually talk to them.
- When you talk to them, don't just ask straightforward questions like "Why do you give?" or "Which offer do you like best?"—come at it with free-flowing questions that get the individual to think at a deeper level. The questions should not be directly about the organization but rather generosity in general or the cause category—questions like "Tell me about a time when you were moved to give."
- Consider having an outside group handle this portion since it can be difficult to filter out our biases and personal experiences with our organizations and brands.

Since then, the team at Sublimity has developed a robust approach to using human-centered design to design various programs.

TAKEAWAY: Don't assume you know what donors will be motivated to give to on a recurring basis. Talk to them. Creating a strong value proposition and a clear identity for your subscription giving program takes a deeper understanding of what motivates your donors and fires their imagination.

While we're on the topic of creating a thriving program based on donor insights, let's discuss crafting an ongoing value proposition.

CHAPTER 23

Craft an Ongoing Value Proposition—Connection with Need

ONE OF THE biggest mistakes nonprofits make today is thinking of recurring giving as a simple offer, a transaction type, or, worse, a checkbox on a website—not a holistic program that needs a clear value proposition, benefits, and a sense of community.

One of the most valuable things you can do to create a thriving sustainer program is to treat it as a holistic program instead of a method of giving.

One of the most valuable things you can do to create a thriving sustainer program is to treat it as a holistic program instead of a method of giving.

This chapter will cover the core elements of designing a thriving giving program with a compelling value proposition.

The first lesson is that recurring giving is a program, not an offer. A strong sustainer program requires more than a checkbox on a website.

Treat Recurring Giving as a Holistic Program

The offer is important, which, in simple language, is a description of what your donor's gift will accomplish. But the offer alone in the subscription economy is not enough. Nor is recurring giving simply a channel, a gift type, or a donor classification. It's so much more.

It's important to think of recurring giving as a holistic program. A holistic recurring giving program starts with a high-quality, ongoing value proposition.

A High-Quality Ongoing-Value Proposition

Tim Kachuriak is the chief innovation and optimization officer and founder of NextAfter, a fundraising research lab and consultancy. He has been a pioneer in helping nonprofit organizations hone and test their value propositions. NextAfter has conducted thousands of tests over a decade and helped hundreds of organizations grow by hundreds of millions of dollars.

I asked Tim to describe his thinking about value propositions. He said, "The value proposition for us in our world is the answer to a very specific question—and it's a question that every single donor has to hear the answer to, but they are never going to ask."

The question is, "If I am your ideal donor, why should I give to you rather than some other organization, or not at all?"

Kachuriak clarifies, "Every organization has a value proposition, but it's not something that you can declare. You can't just go plant a flag and say, 'This is my value proposition.' You have to discover it because it lives inside the hearts and the minds of your existing and potential supporters."

Tim breaks down this critical question, phrase by phrase:

"If I am your ideal donor, why should I give to you rather than some other organization, or not at all?"

"If I ..."

Tim says, "A value proposition must first be framed from not an organizational-centric point of view but a *donor-centric* point of view, which means that you need to start looking at your organization not through your eyes but through the eyes of your customer."

"Am your ideal donor ..."

"Not any donor, but your ideal donor." Tim continues, "What are the people who are really the ideal true believers in our cause? And you have to be willing to make trade-offs, which means in some cases, the expression of your value proposition to the ideal donor will turn off other people who could potentially be donors to your organization."

"Why should I ..."

"The value proposition is begging for you to present an argument. A very effective value proposition always begins with the same word—*because*. Why should I give to you? *Because* ... So what you are doing is you are presenting an argument that is going to resonate with that ideal donor."

"Give to your organization rather than some other organization, or not at all?"

These are the other trade-offs you have to consider. Tim continues, "As much as we don't like to talk about competition in the nonprofit space, the reality is that we are competing for donor dollars from every single nonprofit organization on the planet. But actually, it's even beyond that. It's not just every nonprofit organization; it's every single consumer brand on planet Earth. Because the donor has a choice—they could give to you, they could give to some other organization, *or* they can make the third choice of 'I'm not going to give at all.' And, honestly, most nonprofit organizations never address that final question. Why should I give? What is the benefit to me of actually giving? What is the intangible thing I receive in exchange for my philanthropic gift?"

TAKEAWAY: A strong value proposition clearly articulates to your ideal donors exactly why they should give to your organization rather than some other organization or not at all.

Let's now look at crafting a strong recurring sustainer-giving value proposition.

Crafting a Subscription Giving Value Proposition

Nathan Hill serves as Vice President of the NextAfter Institute. Hill shares four core attributes of a strong value proposition—appeal, clarity, exclusivity, and credibility.

Appeal— The offer must be something that people are attracted to. Is your value proposition attractive to your ideal prospect?

Clarity—How quickly and easily can donors understand what you are asking? Does it make sense? Using clear language helps donors quickly and easily understand your program's value proposition.

Exclusivity—Can the donor create this kind of impact anywhere else? What is unique and compelling about your program that makes it unique and different? Exclusivity can also relate to feelings of specialness and the insider element of being part of an inner core.

Credibility—What reasons are there for donors to trust you or believe your claims? There are many ways to establish credibility, including sharing data to illustrate the impact, donor reviews, testimonials from beneficiaries, and certifications or marks from trusted third parties (such as GuideStar).

Hill goes on to share six steps to write a nonprofit value proposition. Since this process applies to creating a sustainer value proposition, I've included a slightly modified version of it here:[36]

1. Define the Problem Your Organization Exists to Solve

What problem exactly is your organization trying to solve in the world? Is it a problem that your prospective donors will easily recognize? Will they be compelled by this problem and inspired to be a part of the solution? As Hill writes, "If there is no problem to solve, there is no reason to give." It's important to clarify what problem your organization is trying to solve.

2. List Out Your Value Claims—How You Solve the Problem

The next step is to clearly outline the ways in which you are solving the problem. Hill recommends listing as many value claims as you can, involving people from all parts of your organization. Remember that for sustainer programs, the solution needs to have an ongoing component to justify ongoing giving.

3. Evaluate and Prioritize Your Claims

Next, discern which claims you believe are most likely to resonate with potential sustainers. Hill recommends giving each of your value claims a score of one to five on two scales—appeal and exclusivity.

- Appeal—A strong "appeal" means your ideal donor really wants to make this kind of impact.
- Exclusivity—A strong "exclusivity" score means your ideal donor can only make this impact through your organization.

Add up the two and rank the highest-scoring value claims to identify your top ten. The ideal value claims are highly attractive to would-be sustainers and exclusively unique to your organization.

4. Narrow Your Top Claims by Soliciting Donor Feedback

Our best intuition is no substitute for feedback from donors. While you will develop this list of claims internally, it's important to talk to donors.

Hill recommends creating "a survey to see how donors resonate with your top value claims. Give them a chance to share why they give in their own words." I recommend going further and talking to donors in real time. Look for opportunities to connect with donors—at a natural time, like an event, or you may arrange video meetings or phone calls with a handful of donors. Donor feedback is critical all along the way because organizational leaders make assumptions about what they think is valuable to donors.

5. Run Tests to Validate Your Claims

NextAfter is known for running and documenting thousands of A/B tests, raising millions of dollars for charities for over a decade. There is a refined methodology for testing that we won't unpack here, but briefly, the idea is to take concepts and split them into two (or more) treatments. Then, using online testing software, split the traffic/audience and measure the outcomes of each treatment. If you want to learn more about testing the NextAfter way, I'll include a link to NextAfter's recommendations in the notes at the end of this book.[37]

Hill recommends, "Use your survey results to generate hypotheses about what could work to increase giving. Run an A/B test to see what your donors actually give to more."

Remember: your goal is to grow recurring giving, so measure your results in terms of newly acquired or converted recurring donors, average gifts, and long-term value.

When you run tests, pretty much any sustainer acquisition effort will receive one-off gifts. These are great and can help underwrite the sustainer acquisition, but they can cloud results if you focus too much on them when trying to figure out your best subscription giving value proposition.

I will also add that if your organization is small or doesn't have a lot of traffic or a large list, A/B testing can be difficult. This may be due to a lack of technology know-how and not having enough volume of traffic or emails to do the test. In these cases, the best thing you can do is take donor feedback and launch with the messaging you think works best, reevaluating after some time—typically thirty to ninety days.

6. Contextualize Your Value Proposition to Each Audience

The last step is to tailor your value proposition to the particular audience you are communicating with. For example, cold audiences that have never heard of you before will need to be communicated with differently. How can you hook them in a way that makes them immediately recognize the problem and pay attention?

On the other hand, warm audiences have some awareness of you—they might have viewed content you've put in front of them or downloaded a resource. These interested audiences need to be met where they are with a contextualized value proposition tailored to move them deeper into engagement and toward making that sustainer gift.

Still differently, existing single-gift donors need to see your value proposition in the context of supporting the organization. They may *seem* closest to becoming a recurring subscription donor—after all, they've given before. However, existing donors can be some of the toughest to convert to sustaining giving, especially after the first thirty to sixty days of becoming a donor. This may be for several reasons, including the natural patterns and giving habits that donors settle into, which can prove difficult to break. It also could be that the mental model they formed when giving that first one-time gift might counter the mental model conducive to a monthly gift.

We'll wrap up our discussion of crafting an ongoing value proposition with a few thoughts regarding describing the need.

Describing the Need—Survival, Safety, and Belonging

Are you familiar with Maslow's Hierarchy of Needs? First proposed in 1943 by American psychologist Abraham Maslow, his theory of motivation has been popular for decades.

Maslow's hierarchy of needs includes the following five different levels, from high-functioning needs to base needs:[33]

1. **Self-actualization**—Desire to become the most that one can be.
2. **Esteem**—Respect, self-esteem, status, recognition, strength, freedom.
3. **Love and belonging**—Friendship, intimacy, family, sense of connection.
4. **Safety needs**—Personal security, employment, resources, health, property.
5. **Physiological needs**—Air, water, food, shelter, sleep, clothing, reproduction.

When fundraising, your goal should be to express your appeal in terms of the lower-level needs of survival, safety, and belonging.

The premise of the hierarchy of needs is that we all have base needs that dominate our attention and motivation. Until those lower-level needs—such as survival and safety—are satisfied, we cannot move on to higher-functioning needs, like belonging, esteem, and, ultimately, self-actualization.

When fundraising, your goal should be to express your appeal in terms of the lower-level needs of survival, safety, and belonging.

TAKEAWAY: Survival, safety, and belonging look different for every charity and every cause, but the goal should be to help donors see how their ongoing support will provide for the survival, safety, and belonging of others.

Related to appealing to our basic needs, recurring giving is also about cultivating a connection with human need.

Cultivating a Connection with Human Need

Monthly giving is not about giving to provide inanimate *things*, but meeting *people* in their moment of need. Sometimes, the donor's gift will provide for "things," not individual people. For example, I've worked with charities where the primary activity is to build radio towers, truck goods and supplies nationwide, and produce content. In each of these examples, the subscription giving helps make each of these things possible.

Even so, look for ways to describe the human need being met and the humans who will be helped as a result of meeting this need. The extent to which you can cultivate a connection with human needs will help drive success in your program.

Finally, let's look at the inverse of connecting donors with human needs—cultivating a human connection with donors.

Cultivating a Human Connection with Donors

On the other side of connecting donors with human need is making a human connection with donors. Just as donors can give on a recurring basis to enable the survival, safety, and belonging of the charity's beneficiaries, a strong recurring giving program can provide the same for donors.

On the other side of connecting donors with human need is making a human connection with donors.

Consider how your recurring giving program can provide for your donors' survival, safety, and especially belonging. You may not be providing direct services to donors, but you can look for indirect opportunities to provide these things.

For example, donors may give to your charity to indicate to themselves and the world that they identify with the cause. This is a form of belonging. Seth Godin, marketing thought leader and multiple-book author, says it this way: "People like us do things like this."

"People like us do things like this." In other words, giving can be a powerful form of self-expression, of saying, "I belong with, and I identify with this community."

We can also cultivate a human connection with recurring donors by treating them well. This includes how we onboard new sustainers—how can we show that we see and honor them? Do they receive a personal touch? What is our ongoing relationship with them? Do they have an opportunity to engage with us and with the cause directly?

The final area in which we can cultivate human connection with our donors is by understanding their underlying beliefs and motivations, and seeking to meet their needs. We discussed this in the prior chapter.

A core part of the value proposition is an offer that justifies ongoing involvement. Let's look at that next.

CHAPTER 24

Develop Your Offer—Nailing the Essentials

IN CHAPTER 11, we learned an offer is a "simple description of what your donor's gift will accomplish."

A recurring gift is a big commitment. We aren't asking donors just to make an impulse decision to support us one time, but instead to commit to an ongoing donation every month or every year.

The significance of the commitment to subscription giving is such that the fundraising offer for a recurring gift must justify ongoing involvement.

Following is a list of ten questions we need to answer when formulating a compelling recurring gift offer:

1. What inspires the donor?
2. What is the need?
3. How are you solving the problem?
4. Why do you need their *ongoing* support?
5. What will their giving do, specifically?
6. Does it make sense?

7. Is it a good deal?
8. Why act now?
9. What are the consequences of not acting?
10. What incentives are there to act?

As Tim Kachuriak explained in the last chapter, when developing a strong value proposition, we need to answer the question, "If I am your ideal donor, why should I give to you rather than some other organization, or not at all?"

Committing to giving a recurring gift on an ongoing basis is a different decision than making a one-time gift, which can be made on an impulse or in response to a momentary need.

Recurring giving is an ongoing commitment requiring an ongoing value proposition to justify the relationship.

TAKEAWAY: Recurring giving is an ongoing commitment requiring an ongoing value proposition to justify the relationship. Don't assume that your best one-time donation ask is the best ask for recurring giving.

Let's look at how nonprofits can set ask amounts and "price points" for recurring giving.

Offer Price Points and Ask Amounts

The last element of a good offer is related to the ask amount. What will my gift do, and how much will that cost? This begs the question:

Should you set your recurring giving ask amount at a specific dollar amount?

Over the past several decades, many programs have had a fixed price point or ask amount. For example, St. Jude Children's Research Hospital featured $19 a month for their Partners in Hope program. For $39 dollars a month, you could sponsor a child through World Vision.

But today, many organizations don't have a fixed monthly amount. Instead, they have amounts that indicate the impact you can have but then allow the donor to choose the monthly amount they want to give.

Even St. Jude's has broadened the ask amounts, giving examples of what different giving levels can accomplish. For example, consider the following:

- $10 could help provide a new toy for hospital play areas.
- $25 could help provide one day of meals for a patient in the Kay Kafe, the hospital cafeteria.
- $50 could help provide one bone marrow needle for a patient.
- $120 could help provide a red wagon used to transport patients through the hospital.

[Items listed here are representative of services and supplies that are part of the treatment and care of children at St. Jude. The cost of each item or service is an approximation and will vary based on actual costs incurred and individual patient needs. Your donation will be used for the general operating needs of St. Jude, where no family ever receives a bill for treatment, travel housing, or food so they can focus on helping their child live.]

The copy clarifies that these are approximate amounts meant to illustrate the kinds of impact you can have at different giving levels.

St. Jude's illustrates the impact of different giving amounts by giving donors a choice that correlates to varying levels of impact.

The principle is to inspire donors to see the kinds of impact they can make at different giving levels and let them choose the amount based on their own ability and comfort level.

One benefit of empowering donors to give at the level they are comfortable with is higher giving amounts. Instead of pushing donors to give at a lower level that represents the most common denominator, donors who can choose their own amount often give at higher levels. I know nonprofits with donors who give $1,000, $2,500, or more monthly. That's because that's what these donors are comfortable with and capable of. I wouldn't want to push them to give $38 a month, if they can give at a more significant level.

The principle is to inspire donors to see the kinds of impact they can make at different giving levels

The other benefit of not having a fixed monthly gift amount is that it makes upgrading donors more flexible and easier. You can periodically ask donors to increase their gift amounts in whatever increments they are comfortable with. Some donors may add five dollars to their recurring gift amount, while others may add fifteen dollars or fifty dollars. The donor can choose to increase their giving to whatever level they are comfortable with rather than having to move in increments of thirty-eight dollars or whatever.

There are still some sustainer programs where a fixed price per subscription makes sense, such as with child sponsorship, but many nonprofits today don't need a single price point for their monthly giving program. The opportunity to encourage donors to give far more than that fixed amount outweighs the potential benefits of sticking with a fixed amount.

The Role of Anchoring in Ask Amounts

The last thing we should cover related to ask amounts is the principle of price anchoring. According to Zerocap in an article titled "What Is Price Anchoring?", anchoring is "a cognitive bias that refers to the human tendency to rely too heavily on the first piece of information offered when making decisions. In pricing, the initial price sets the stage for customer expectations and comparisons."[39]

In pricing, anchoring refers to what you lead with and how you set expectations with consumers or donors.

In subscription giving, if you start the conversation with "for $5/month," you've anchored the donor at a $5/month starting point. Price anchoring tells us that if, for example, we start at $5/month a donor will be less likely to give an amount like $100/month, because we "anchored" them at such a low amount.

One way to use price anchoring to positive effect is to plant seeds for larger gift amounts. You could say something like, "Our most faithful supporters give sacrificially. To some, that might be $100 a month, while to others, it might be $10 monthly, and still others, $1,000 a month." By starting with a higher amount, you "anchor" what tends to stick in the donors' minds while giving them options that are both lower and higher.

One way to use price anchoring to positive effect is to plant seeds for larger gift amounts.

TAKEAWAY: Anchoring is an important concept to help donors see the difference their gift can make and understand the impact of different levels of giving.

Let's now look at gift frequency as it relates to recurring giving.

Subscription Giving and Recurring Gift Frequency

As with consumer subscriptions, recurring gifts vary in frequency, typically between monthly, quarterly, and annually. While monthly frequency is the most popular option, increasing numbers of nonprofits offer alternative frequencies.

For example, in face-to-face fundraising, where churn can be higher in the first couple of months, there is a case to be made for a quarterly frequency, ensuring fewer but larger gifts from donors and longer retention.

> Charities are increasingly experimenting with alternative recurring gift frequencies such as quarterly and annual recurring giving.

Charities are increasingly experimenting with annual gift frequency—for example, a single annual gift that is automated as a recurring gift. When I first heard of this, I thought, "Isn't that essentially the same as a single-gift donor? Why would you allow such an infrequent gift amount?"

But think about it—many donors have a pattern of giving seasonally, just once a year. Think of organizations like Union Rescue Mission, which we discussed in chapter 11. Human services organizations like URM see the highest level of giving and engagement during the Thanksgiving and Christmas seasons, including many donors who only give one gift per year. Suppose you could target and convert those types of seasonal or occasional donors and get them to sign up for an automated gift annually. In that case, you will increase donor retention year over year.

We also know from other gift frequencies that recurring donors are often the most likely to give another gift to the organization—typically an additional 25 percent on top of their recurring giving in the case of monthlies. So, if donors commit to a single annual recurring gift, it stands to reason that they would be more likely to give additional gifts.

While further testing is needed for alternative frequencies, such as quarterly and annual recurring giving, the options show promise.

TAKEAWAY: A strong recurring giving offer not only justifies ongoing involvement but also includes a variety of price points, ask amounts, and alternative frequencies.

While an ongoing value proposition and a strong offer are essential to success, a holistic recurring giving program also includes several other elements.

Next, let's look at one of the most critical considerations in setting up your recurring giving program for scale and success—the technology that enables everything.

CHAPTER 25

Get Your Tech Stack Right—Systems and Platforms

YOUR SYSTEMS AND platforms will either be your biggest limiting factor or your best ally in scaling your subscription giving program.

> Your systems and platforms will either be your biggest limiting factor or your best ally in scaling your subscription giving program.

In this chapter, we'll define recurring subscription giving technology and discuss the various platforms involved with any recurring giving system.

The technologies that come together to make subscription giving possible are commonly referred to as a "tech stack." A subscription giving tech stack involves three types of building blocks—back-end, front-end, and middleware.

Back-end technologies are behind the scenes and form a stable base for the stack, where all mission-critical data and technology lies. Front-end technologies involve everything that drives what your users see and interact with. And finally, middleware connects it all, helping data flow from one place to another and identifying insights and opportunities.

Note that some technologies can serve multiple functions that overlap with one another. For example, your nonprofit CRM database may be able to send emails—a function that an email marketing platform can do as well. We won't get into all of the nuances of deciding which tool should do which job in this case. I will say, however, that I tend to prefer fewer tools as long as you aren't making significant sacrifices in capabilities to give your donors a great experience.

TAKEAWAY: The technologies that power recurring giving together form the subscription giving tech stack and are made up of back-end, front-end, and middleware.

Let's list and review the different technologies that make up the building blocks of the subscription giving tech stack.

Nonprofit CRM or Donor Management System

Your CRM or donor database is the most fundamental building block—it's where charities store information about supporters. CRM usually stands for customer relationship management, but in the nonprofit world, it refers to constituents such as donors, subscribers, volunteers, and so on.

A good CRM manages donor information, tracks donations, segments donors for targeted campaigns, and maintains communications history. Ideally, the CRM also tracks all nondonors, such as subscribers and volunteers.

Since this is your central storehouse, it should have as much data as possible on your constituents and how they interact with you. At a minimum, CRMs typically contain donation transactional data, but ideally, your CRM would also have other data like email engagement, volunteerism, expressed interests, and so on. Many CRMs integrate with other tools in the tech stack, such as online donations, e-commerce, email marketing, marketing automation, and more.

Mark Becker is a founding partner at Cathexis Partners, a firm that helps nonprofits set up and use technology to raise funds and engage with supporters more effectively. Over the past fifteen years, Mark and his team have helped hundreds of organizations find and implement technology solutions.

Mark says he's seen a significant increase in nonprofits prioritizing recurring giving as they consider CRM solutions. "It's really important. And the solutions are doing a better job of making it very easy to convert from someone who was considering being a one-time donor to a monthly sustained giver instead and making that process as seamless as possible."

Becker says that most tech-stack decisions start with the nonprofit's CRM—"It always starts with, OK, what's your CRM? And then let's see what tools we can get that either come with it or can hook into it."

There are dozens of nonprofit CRMs out there, which is why it's so important to spend time understanding your needs before deciding on whether to stay or switch to another provider.

> Your CRM is the most crucial technology decision you will ever make, so it's worth spending the time to ensure you are on the right platform.

Some CRMs are better for larger organizations with more complex needs, while others are great for smaller charities. The CRM is the most crucial tech-stack decision you will ever make, and it is the hardest to change, so it's worth spending the time to ensure you are on the right platform.

Donation Processor

The next element to the back end of your recurring giving tech stack is your transaction or gift processing. This might include whomever you use to handle your offline check processing, but since recurring giving is predominantly via credit card, ACH, or other digital payment methods, we're primarily focused on digital payments.

Sometimes, your CRM or your donation platform (which we'll cover next) determines who your gift processor is. They will often have integrated a payment processor into their solution—just know this is a separate technology from your CRM or donation platform.

Becker says the one critical thing with your transaction processor is to make sure they have a process for migrating secure tokens. Tokens are the security pieces of data that enable automated payments to occur.

I've heard horror stories about nonprofits who were not able to migrate tokens for existing recurring donors, and they effectively had to re-recruit existing donors, losing many of them in the process.

"If a nonprofit is planning on moving, make sure there's a clear process for migrating those tokens so you don't lose too many in the process," Mark says. "When you move systems, the first key is to make sure you're working with a platform that is good at breakups and doesn't want to hold your data hostage, including your tokens, because the previous merchant service has to release the tokens."

Becker continues that you should look to your provider to advise you on the communication strategy to donors around such a transition: "You also need to have a built-in communication saying, 'Hey, we're changing our payment processor. Your receipts are going to be changing.' So there's the whole communication strategy around that."

TAKEAWAY: The nonprofit CRM and donation processor are two of the most critical technologies in the subscription giving tech stack and two of the most difficult to replace. While any tool can be swapped out over time, these are the two technologies that are the most painful to change and, therefore, the two most important to get right in the first place.

Now, let's turn to the front end of the subscription giving stack.

Donation Platform

The donation platform powers online donation tools and enables you to accept donations through your website. This is the technology that donors interact with when they sign up for giving or update their giving status.

Your donation platform is the most crucial element of your front end because it influences the donor experience the most. An easy-to-use and intuitive front-end donation experience is essential to maximizing subscription giving.

An easy-to-use and intuitive front-end donation experience is essential to maximizing subscription giving.

TAKEAWAY: If the CRM and donation processor are the two most important technologies powering your subscription giving program, then the donation platform is in the top three. It forms the foundation of the donor experience.

Email Marketing Software

Email marketing tools, often called email service providers (ESPs), help you send email newsletters, appeals, and so on. A good email marketing platform enables templates, tracking, and triggered communications and includes robust analytics. Often, other tools such as your CRM or marketing automation software will have email marketing capabilities integrated into it.

The most crucial channel for communicating with prospects and recurring donors today is email.

The most crucial channel for communicating with prospects and recurring donors today is email. Despite the advent of social media, mobile messaging, direct messaging, mobile apps, and so on, it still comes back to the foundation of being able to send emails to donors and prospects. Because of this, your choice of email marketing software is critical.

Mobile Messaging

Increasingly, nonprofits connect with donors and prospects through mobile apps and messaging. Similar to email marketing tools, there are often dedicated tools that enable mobile messaging with donors and constituents. Like with email marketing software, sometimes other tools have this functionality built in, such as a CRM or email marketing software.

Tools to Connect Platforms or Data

The beauty of technology in the twenty-first century is that most platforms enable different ways to sync data or trigger actions using tools called APIs or other middleware.

For example, Zapier is a web-based automation tool that connects different apps, services, and platforms to automate tasks and workflows without needing any coding skills.[40] It allows users to create "Zaps," automated workflows linking two or more apps together. For example, you can create a Zap that automatically saves new email signups into your CRM and triggers a welcome email. Zapier supports integration with thousands of popular apps, making it a versatile tool for streamlining processes and increasing productivity. Zapier is just one example of a middleware tool that helps connect data and functions between tools.

Data Analytics and Reporting

Understanding your fundraising data and subscription giving performance is critical. Analytics tools can help you track the performance of your campaigns, report on, and better understand donor behavior.

We discussed measurement and reporting in chapter 20, but to do that, you need tools for measurement and reporting. Analytics tools can help you track the performance of your campaigns and understand owner behavior.

TAKEAWAY: Making the right decisions about the technology that powers your subscription giving program and implementing them well will either be the biggest barrier to growth or enable you to scale to new heights.

Note that this is not a comprehensive list of technology tools such as internal collaboration, social media management, and creative and content production. Because these tools are not specific to subscription giving, we won't address them here.

The four fundamental technologies are your CRM, donation processor, donation platform, and email marketing provider.

The most fundamental pieces of technology that need to support your ability to grow your program are your CRM, donation processor, donation platform, and email marketing software.

Now that we've described the tech stack and understood its individual components, let's look at the considerations for any modern subscription giving tech stack.

Tech-Stack Considerations for Recurring Giving

As we conclude this chapter, let's look at six core considerations when building or evaluating the technology that empowers recurring giving in your organization:

1. Ease of Use
2. Customer Experience

3. Capability
4. Scalability
5. Integration
6. Automation

Let's start with the ease of use of the technology internally.

Ease of Use

The first consideration is ease of use. If set up properly and with limited training, can the people using the system do so easily and efficiently? Or, by contrast, does your technology require highly specialized and advanced training? Similarly, can many people use it at least at an intermediate or expert level, or can only one person?

By the way, I'm not saying your tools should be "so easy that a monkey can use them." There will always be some level of training required to use these systems well.

Note that sometimes "ease of use" can be translated into "basic" or "not very powerful." Often, the more powerful a technology is, the more advanced users need to utilize it. There is a tension between ease of use and power or sophistication. But this is not always the case. Sometimes, technology can be complicated and not very powerful because it's dated or not well-designed.

But if your people can't use a technology because it's difficult or convoluted or because only one highly technical person can do anything, you've got a problem. Any time you have a single point of failure or unnecessary friction in using a tool, you waste time and money and can hurt the donor experience.

TAKEAWAY: As you explore different tools, consider the potential tension between ease of use and capabilities. With training, your technology should be usable by the team members who need to use it. Having only one or a few staff members who can effectively use your tools is a significant risk.

Customer Experience

As you examine your technology and systems, the next consideration is how each impacts the customer experience. While this includes front-end systems where donors and end users interact directly with the technology, such as your website or donation forms, it also relates to back-end systems, which can make the donor experience either better or worse.

For example, suppose your donation processor cannot auto-update credit cards when issued a new expiration date. In that case, you've just made the donor experience worse, even though the donor doesn't interact directly with your donation processor.

The tools you choose have a major impact on the experience you deliver for donors.

The most important front-end experience is donor sign-up and onboarding. Sign-up should be smooth and easy—forms and landing pages should be joys for end users to interact with, and donors should be communicated with in a timely manner.

TAKEAWAY: The tools you choose have a major impact on the experience you deliver for donors. Make sure to use tools that will improve and enhance the donor experience.

Capabilities

The next area to look at when choosing technology is capability. The capabilities you need from any technology will change as your program matures, but all platforms should be capable of doing what you need.

For example, a donation platform or gift processor should have a good process around credit card declines, notifications, and the capability to enable automated credit card retries with payment processors. Every organization will have nuances, which means that all organizations have different requirements.

Every organization has different requirements; it is important to get clear about those requirements when evaluating or searching for solutions.

I recommend documenting the requirements of what you need from any piece of your technology before you search for a solution, including when you are considering evaluating your existing solution.

TAKEAWAY: The tools you choose must be capable of doing what you need. Every organization has different requirements; it is important to get clear about those requirements when evaluating or searching for solutions.

Scalability

Will your technology and processes hold up at twice your current size? How about ten times your current size? How about fifty times?

You might have processes and platforms that work well for you today, but will they work well for you as you grow?

A common mistake that organizations make when choosing technology is that they select technology that works well for them today based on the size and complexity of their program.

They may consider what might happen if the program scales one to two times, but a well-designed and executed subscription giving program will grow far beyond that. Will each tool in your tech stack work well at ten times or fifty times the current size? What systems and platforms might break? You'll want to consider this when making decisions, considering how difficult that technology will be to replace as you grow.

Don't underestimate what is possible in ten years, especially regarding more critical technology solutions like your CRM and donation processor.

Bill Gates famously said, "Most people overestimate what they can do in one year and underestimate what they can do in ten years." Don't underestimate what is possible in ten years, especially regarding more critical technology solutions like your CRM and donation processor.

TAKEAWAY: For each element of your tech stack, ask yourself, will this solution serve us well at ten times our current scale? Fifty times? Use your answers to inform your decisions.

Integration with Other Solutions

Broadly speaking, there are two kinds of tech solutions—all-in-one and point solutions.

An all-in-one solution fills many functions within your technology stack—it might serve as your donor database of record (CRM), email service provider, automation tool, front-end donation platform, and others.

On the other hand, a point solution might serve just one or two functions well—such as your email and marketing automation needs. The point solution is also referred to as "best-in-breed," meaning they might do one or two functions super well.

The trade-off between choosing an all-in-one solution versus point solutions is that point solutions need to be integrated with other solutions. Integration typically is in the form of data flowing from one system to another.

Thankfully, many point solutions know that they live or die on their ability to integrate well with other solutions, and so have integrations built with many different tools. You want to ensure that any point solution you choose can integrate well with other tools, particularly your CRM.

At the same time, all-in-one solutions can eliminate the sometimes arduous task of integrating data and tools.

There is no easy answer, which is why it's so important to document your technical requirements before looking for solutions or when evaluating existing solutions.

Another trade-off to consider is the size of your team. The smaller your team, the more valuable it is to have fewer solutions built to work together.

TAKEAWAY: Whether you go with an all-in-one solution or multiple best-in-class point solutions, you'll want to consider your requirements and how you'll integrate data and processes to create the best experience and reduce extra work.

Automation

Ask yourself, how much manual work will be required to operate this platform or technology? What is possible to automate once you have your systems figured out?

For example, with an email platform, how much can it be automated, such as sending triggered emails based on the donor behavior?

How about the data flow between systems? Can it be automated, or will someone have to download/upload data manually on a regular basis?

If a donor has a change in giving, such as a credit card decline, is an automated triggered email sent to them immediately?

TAKEAWAY: Proper automation can save time and improve the donor experience. Consider what steps and processes you can automate when choosing or evaluating tools.

Now that we've laid the foundation of the technology that powers recurring giving, we will examine what it takes to grow a sustainer program: acquisition and conversion.

CHAPTER 26

Design and Launch (or Relaunch)—Program Design

IN ADDITION TO a strong offer and ongoing value proposition, a holistic subscription giving program includes a clear brand identity, benefits, and a dedicated presence.

A Clear Brand Identity

The next thing to consider as you develop a holistic subscription giving program is a clear identity. Every subscription giving program should have a brand, something that gives it a sense of identity.

A clear brand identity starts with a name.

Naming Subscription Giving Programs

One of the most common questions with sustainer programs is whether they should have a unique name. Does your recurring giving program need a special name, or does naming even matter?

As Shakespeare wisely penned many years ago, "What's in a name? That which we call a rose by any other name would smell as sweet."

Does it even matter if one's subscription giving program has a unique name? It is difficult to isolate a name's impact on the success of a recurring giving program.

Based on my research, I will say, yes, you should have a name for your subscription giving program. There are a few reasons for this.

Reasons for a Named Subscription Giving Program

The first reason is a practical matter—a unique program name makes it easy to refer to the program in a distinct way. This reduces the chance of confusion when you refer to your recurring donors and the program itself. If a charity says, "Thank you for being a faithful donor," that could mean a number of things. But if the charity says, "Thank you for being a Child Sponsor," or "a member of The Spring," or "a Humane Hero," or "a Freedom Partner," it's clear you're talking about a specific program and not just donors in general.

The second reason for a unique program name is that it creates a sense of identity and belonging, which benefits both the charity and the donor. The expression of identity has always played an important role in philanthropy, whether that be the earliest examples of the Jewish people giving their first fruits as part of what it meant to be a part of that community, or in the eighteenth century, a patron of the arts giving as an expression of belonging to that community, or any other cause today. As discussed in chapter 8, the notion that "people like us do things like this" is a powerful force of group identity.

The third reason to consider a named recurring gift program is the ability to enhance its value proposition. If I ask you, "Would you become a monthly donor?" that is pretty straightforward. But if I say, "Would you become a member of Flight Crew and stand with us monthly?" there is a higher sense of value. A unique subscription giving program name can contribute to a feeling of increased value and impact.

A unique subscription giving program name can contribute to a feeling of increased value and impact.

TAKEAWAY: A unique sustainer program name not only helps with language, making it clear when referring to a sustainer program, but it also can create a sense of identity and belonging and increase perceived value to donors.

There are two different approaches that charities can take when naming a subscription giving program.

Sustainer Program Naming—Two Approaches

The first approach to naming a program is descriptive. "Descriptive" names simply describe what they are in more straightforward terms.

Descriptive naming conventions often include modifier words like Sponsor, Partner, Friend, Member, Builder, Defender, Club, Advocate,

Associate, Champion, and so on. Examples of descriptively named recurring giving programs include the following:

- St. Jude Children's Research Hospital has *Partners in Hope.*
- Red Cross has *Red Cross Champions.*
- International Justice Mission has *Freedom Partners.*
- The Humane Society of the United States has *Humane Heroes.*
- Ducks Unlimited has *Wetlands Champions.*
- World Wildlife Fund has *WWF Heroes.*

The second approach to naming a subscription giving program is fanciful.

Fanciful sustainer program names are either invented words or combinations of existing words that form a new meaning, word picture, or metaphor. Examples in the nonprofit world of recurring giving programs with fanciful names include these:

- charity: water has *The Spring.*
- Mission Aviation Fellowship has *Flight Crew.*
- Pencils of Promise has *Passport.*
- Life House Ministries has *The Village.*
- To Write Love On Her Arms has *TWLOHA Blue.*
- Save the Children has *Team Tomorrow.*

Both approaches have downsides to manage along with their strengths.

For descriptively named programs, be careful to avoid generic names or names that are not memorable or distinctive. At a minimum, include the organization's name with a modifier to make it specific. For example, Heifer International's program is called Friends of Heifer. Red Cross has Red Cross Champions.

You want donors to be able to remember and recognize it when you refer to them. If you just say Monthly Partners, for example, that name is not memorable or distinctive to your organization or cause.

For fanciful program names, be careful not to be too obscure or too insider-focused. Sometimes nonprofit leaders can be overly clever when naming their program, and donors have trouble remembering the name. Sometimes a name can be too "inside baseball" when it refers to some part of your program or something you're proud of but that the general public or donor population would not understand unless explained to them.

> Sustainer program names can be either fanciful or descriptive. Either way, they should be memorable, insightful, and not cause confusion.

As an example to avoid, some nonprofits will name their program with a series of numbers or some obscure turn of phrase in a foreign language. While the concept may be very appealing to insiders at the organization, donors don't understand or remember such obscure references. When donors can't quickly understand a concept or it doesn't make any sense to outsiders, it can cause confusion and lack of memorability.

There is no clear evidence of whether a fanciful name is better than a more descriptive name. But given our research, I believe it's important to have a unique name for your program. When you use it, people understand what you are referring to.

TAKEAWAY: Your sustainer program should have a unique name. Whether that name is descriptive or fanciful depends on you, your organization's brand, and the insights you glean from your donors. Just be careful not to create confusion about what the organization does or be too insider-focused.

The next element of a clear brand identity for a subscription giving program is a distinct visual identity.

Creating a Distinct Visual Identity

Your program should also have a visual identity related to your organization. It may be part of your charity's visual identity or have its own subbrand. Any visual identity you create for your sustainer program should relate to the parent organization. In other words, it should not be mistaken for another nonprofit. Make sure that it relates to your nonprofit's brand identity.

> Any visual identity you create for your sustainer program should relate to the parent organization.

There's a lot of leeway here, so you can go with something straightforward and descriptive from a visual perspective and duplicate your existing nonprofit brand identity.

Likewise, you can create something more creative and visionary, but there are a few considerations. First, any logo or mark you create for a recurring giving program should relate to the parent brand. Most organizations don't create a unique logo for their recurring giving program, but if you do, you don't want your program to be mistaken for a separate nonprofit.

Second, the style—colors, messaging, and typography—should clearly connect to the parent brand. What you're trying to say is that your monthly giving donors are the core of those making a difference for the cause.

If in doubt, make the visual identity part of the parent organization's visual identity. For an example of a sustainer program associated with its parent brand, look at the Humane Society of the United States' *Humane Heroes* program.

On the other hand, for an example of a fanciful name and unique identity, look at organizations like charity: water's *The Spring* or Mission Aviation Fellowship's *Flight Crew*.

TAKEAWAY: The visual identity for your sustainer program should relate to the overall brand of the charity. It may have a distinct subbrand, logo, and visual palette, but it should be clearly associated with the parent organization. This ensures that there won't be confusion and builds brand recognition for both the program and organization.

After a clear brand identity, the next element of a holistic recurring giving program is to consider benefits.

Subscription Giving Program Benefits

Each organization should consider the benefits that exist for recurring donors who participate in the program.

Donors often receive intangible benefits, such as exclusive content. Such content may include behind-the-scenes stories, unique newsletters, special downloads, and video or audio resources.

Amy Konary from the Subscribed Institute told me, “One of the outcomes is access, for example, and being able to access products or services that you wouldn’t be able to access any other way.”

Each organization should consider the benefits that exist for recurring donors who participate in the program.

While the benefits of subscription giving are most often intangible, there are times when tangible benefits make sense.

Tangible benefits make sense if you offer goods, services, events, or programming. These can be great to bundle together or add exclusive bonuses for faithful supporters—things like access to educational programming, discounts, event invitations, or identity-related swag.

A special note on identity-related swag—it seems most of the time, branded hats, shirts, and so on are of limited value. But if your organization represents a cause with which donors want to associate publicly, consider leaning more toward opportunities to provide identity-related swag, such as pins, bracelets, labels, membership cards, and apparel.

TAKEAWAY: Benefits for recurring donors include intangible resources such as exclusive content or tangible benefits like goods, services, events, or programming. Each organization differs and should tailor its benefits to the donors who identify with the cause.

Now, let’s turn to a dedicated presence—the final element of a holistic, recurring giving program.

A Dedicated Presence in All Communications

Your recurring giving program online should not exist as simply a button on your website or a checkbox on your main donation page. A holistic subscription giving program includes a dedicated presence on the website and other communications and materials.

A Dedicated Website Presence

A subscription giving program starts with a landing page or small section of the website. This is the primary place where prospective subscription donors find out about your program—the need, the offer, the benefits—and are encouraged to sign up.

More advanced programs will have multiple landing pages corresponding to different channels, strategies, and creative approaches that drive traffic to the website.

For example, suppose you are running a specific campaign for recurring giving with a concrete goal, a particular story you are leading with, and even campaign-specific incentives such as a match. In that case, you'll want to have a specific campaign landing page. Otherwise, you risk losing donors due to the friction and anxiety that is produced when the destination doesn't fit the journey.

> A holistic subscription giving program includes a dedicated presence on the website and other communications and materials.

While the program should have a "home base" on the website in the form of landing pages or a section, it should be promoted throughout the website. Multiple calls to action to join the program should exist, starting on the home page.

While it's not true that the homepage of a website is the only page people first visit, it is generally the most visited page of a website. At a minimum, I recommend having a dedicated button to give monthly, once again sending the signal that our monthly donors are the core of our charity. Ideally, charities should have a section of the home page dedicated to your program that briefly describes the impact that donors can have and positions it as a core part of the way the charity is able to do its work.

Also, consider including content throughout the site, such as stories, articles, and videos with a call to action to join the program.

Prominent links throughout the website should cross-promote recurring giving in relevant places. For example, wherever there is content on the site connected to monthly support, include a call to action. That might be on the About page, for example, or where you might have stories or blog posts related to the work you do. Having a call to action around monthly giving to support can be very helpful, making that kind of impact possible.

Include monthly giving calls to action and options on all single-gift donation forms. Ideally, include a graphic or callout that highlights monthly giving, along with the reasons why it is important. An even better strategy can be an incentive or other unique reason for donors to choose to select monthly giving now.

Include an FAQ section on the website about your sustainer program. Answer common questions about how the impact is calculated, cancellation processes, how to update donation information, and so on. You can also sprinkle in reasons to give and donors' impact throughout this type of content.

The recurring donation sign-up process should make the case for recurring giving and, in some cases, may reside right on your sustainer program landing page. Ask for minimal information during the sign-up donation process and affirm the donor's decision.

One reason a dedicated recurring giving donation sign-up process is important is that it signals to would-be donors that recurring giving is a core part of your organization's support structure and not an afterthought or a checkbox on a website.

TAKEAWAY: A dedicated website presence is core to a holistic sustainer program. It signals the importance of recurring giving to your audience, drives awareness of the program, and provides easy ways to join.

A sustainer program doesn't just exist online. Let's look at areas where your dedicated presence can exist in communications and collateral.

Other Communications and Materials

Every organization has a different set of communications and collateral materials. For your charity, consider all of the different communications you produce and ask, "How can we integrate subscription giving program here?"

Let's look at some examples with suggestions.

- **Newsletters**: Sidebar calls to action or stories illustrating donors who have committed to the program or need stories.
- **Direct Mail Appeals**: Include an option to sign up for the program and periodically incentivize conversion to recurring giving.

- **Email**: Depending on the nature of the email, this might range from referencing the program in passing to dedicated recruitment emails. But consider in your non-recruitment emails what place your program might have in other emails.
- **Receipt Inserts**: One of the best places to describe your program and encourage people to join is when affirming them for their last (or first) gift.
- **Mobile Messaging:** If you have a text messaging program or a mobile app, consider ways to include recurring giving.
- **Giving Brochures**: Good old-fashioned collateral can be helpful if you have in-person environments to distribute collateral, such as a volunteer center or facility.
- **Event Collateral:** Consider ways to integrate your program into events.

TAKEAWAY: If your sustainer program is a core part of your organization or you would like it to be, then it should have a presence in all places where it makes sense, both offline and online.

Let's look next at designing—or more likely, redesigning—your sustainer program for success.

CHAPTER 27

Grow Your Program—Recruit Everywhere

THERE ARE TWO ways to grow the number of recurring subscription giving donors. The first is to attract new donors who start as recurring, also known as acquisition. The second is to convert existing one-time donors to recurring, referred to as conversion.

Leaders inevitably ask me, "Which should I focus on for my nonprofit—acquiring new recurring donors or converting existing one-time donors?"

The answer is a resounding "It depends!"

It depends on the kind of recurring giving program you have, how big your current one-time donor file is, what your offer and ongoing value proposition is, and what kind of strategies work for you in acquisition.

Let me share some common traits I see among organizations that see more success in acquiring new recurring donors versus converting existing ones and vice versa.

Acquisition-Focused Organizations

Organizations with most of their new recurring donors coming from acquisition typically have some way of getting in front of audiences at scale and inspiring them to sign up for recurring giving on the spot. Channels capable of larger scale include events, face-to-face, digital, and television.

Organizations that drive significant sustainer acquisition have an offer and value proposition that is highly visible, broadly appealing, has a clear solution, and justifies ongoing giving.

Acquisition-focused organizations have an offer that is highly visible, broadly appealing, has a clear solution, and justifies ongoing giving.

Let's break down each of the elements for a strong acquisition offer and value proposition:

Highly Visible Need: A need the donor can see that is clear and easily understandable. For example, Operation Smile addresses a highly visible need—addressing cleft lip and cleft palate to breathe better, eat, speak, and live lives of greater confidence.

Broad Appeal: When getting in front of large numbers of people, the offer needs to be widely appealing—something that resonates with many people. Going wide to a big audience can be wasteful if your offer is only of interest to a narrow niche. For example, the Humane Society of the United States protects animals and works to end suffering—an admirable endeavor that is widely appealing to many people.

Clear Solution: The solution doesn't require significant education, and the donor can easily see the connection between their giving and making a difference. For example, at charity: water, the solution is clear—they want to bring clean and safe water to every person on the planet.

Justifies Ongoing Giving: There should be some natural reason why the donor's gift is needed on an ongoing basis. For example, at organizations like Save the Children or Compassion International, the nature of child sponsorship justifies ongoing giving. Each month, you can help meet the needs of your sponsored child and their community.

TAKEAWAY: Organizations that see large numbers of new recurring donors have a large-scale way of getting in front of audiences and inspiring them to sign up for recurring giving on the spot, combined with a compelling offer that has a visible need, broad appeal, clear solution, and justifies ongoing giving.

Next, let's look at organizations that see most of their new sustainers coming from existing donors—conversion.

Conversion-Focused Organizations

In my experience, most nonprofits are primarily focused on the conversion of existing donors to grow their sustainer programs.

Conversion-focused organizations have healthy one-time donor acquisition, an existing file, and regular opportunities to be in front of donors.

Many nonprofits have invested extensively over time in building donor files consisting of one-time donors. These charities then tend to seek most of their recurring donors from the conversion of existing donors.

Organizations that focus more on sustainer conversion of existing donors have an existing donor file, a healthy source of one-time donor acquisition, opportunities to be in front of donors, and an offer that is less conducive to acquisition.

Let's break down each of the elements for a strong donor-conversion value proposition:

Existing Donor File: The first thing that charities who see success in donor conversion have is a large enough pool of donors from which to convert. Often, these organizations have built donor files over a period of years.

Healthy Source of One-Time Donor Acquisition: These organizations ideally have a healthy source of new one-time donor acquisition, which becomes a robust feeder of new donors to invite to subscription giving.

Opportunities to Be in Front of Donors: The charity has existing ways to be in front of donors regularly, likely in the form of an ongoing cultivation program for single-gift donors—appeals, newsletters, email, and phone, but also potentially in other ways, such as content or programming, events, and so on.

Offer That Is Less Conducive to Acquisition: This is a little trickier to describe, but imagine any offer that lacks more than one or two components of a successful subscription giving acquisition offer discussed before—highly visible, broadly appealing, has a clear solution, and justifies ongoing giving. If the subscription giving offer lacks multiple of these, then it may take more time for would-be donors to warm up to giving on a recurring basis.

But how do you know when a particular channel may be good for acquisition or conversion?

Evaluating Acquisition and Conversion Channels

Next we'll review a list of channels that are used when acquiring and converting subscription donors. When evaluating options, there are three factors that should play into the decision:

Scale: What is the potential scale of this channel? Can we get a significant volume of subscription giving donors via this channel?

Cost: What is the cost of acquiring sustainers from this channel per new sustainer, and in terms of overall investment?

Value: How valuable is this channel in terms of the long-term value (LTV) of new donors?

There are many different channels that can be used to drive acquisition and conversion. The following table lists seventeen channels, including an A, where they are typically associated with acquisition, and a C, where they are associated with conversion. Some channels will have both.

Events (A,C)	Email (C)	Peer-to-Peer (A)
Website (A,C)	Social Media (A,C)	Text/Mobile (C)
Artists (A)	Digital Media (A,C)	Receipt Inserts (C)
Video/TV (A,C)	Content/Earned Media (A,C)	Collateral (A,C)
Face-to-Face (A)	Search (A,C)	Corporate/Church Relations (A)
Direct Mail (C)		
Phone (C)		

I've included a brief description of each channel and how it's typically used in an addendum at the end of the book.

As you consider each channel, I highly recommend using the impact-effort matrix we discussed in chapter 18. It's a great tool to filter through and prioritize efforts.

Let's look at the other way to grow your subscription giving base: converting existing single-gift donors to recurring donors.

Three Strategies for Conversion

Broadly speaking, there are three categories of strategies to convert existing single-gift donors to subscription giving.

1. Onboarding
2. Always On
3. Episodic

The best window to convert an existing one-time donor is when they are new to the organization, so we'll look at that first.

Onboarding Conversion Strategies

The most likely time for a single-gift donor to give is in the first thirty to sixty days following their first gift.

The most likely time for a single-gift donor to give is in the first thirty to sixty days following their first gift. From my research, I believe this is because of the heightened donor interest right after making the initial decision to support the cause financially, as well as the fact that the donor has not yet settled into a routine of giving. Donors tend to get into patterns of giving, but they have not yet formed those patterns in the first thirty to sixty days, making them more open to a recurring giving relationship.

Whatever the reason, the highest likelihood of conversion is in the first sixty days of a donor giving their first gift to the organization.

Conversion begins before the first gift. The ideal time to start cultivating a recurring gift is before a donor even gives their first single gift. Prospective donors should be aware from the outset that recurring giving is a core part of accomplishing your mission as an organization.

The recurring program should be prominently displayed on your website, discussed in communications, and generally positioned as the foundation upon which you can rely to power your organization's impact month in and month out.

Conversion can take place at the point of the first gift. Donation pages should make recurring giving prominent. Some organizations will offer a pop-up during the donation checkout process, inviting the donor to change their gift to recurring, along with a rationale as to why it is better for donors and for the organization.

Also, some organizations change the default selected giving type on donation forms to monthly. If you do this, ensure it is very clearly highlighted, and include a rationale as to why recurring giving is the best way to ensure that their impact continues. Make sure your thank-you page and receipt email clearly state the recurring giving commitment so donors can modify it if they didn't intend to sign up for recurring. Some nonprofits will call and thank new recurring donors—partly to affirm them and partly to address any cancellations should donors not intend to sign up for recurring.

During the first thirty days, your mission in onboarding new single-gift donors should be twofold—affirming them and inviting them to participate in recurring giving.

The first priority in onboarding is affirming the donor and reporting back on their giving. The most important thing a donor needs before they're ready to make another gift is gratitude and clarity on how their last gift made a difference.

After affirming new donors, the next priority should be to invite them to consider giving on a recurring basis, multiple times, both directly and indirectly.

The goal is to start with the difference they've made as a new donor. Then, we establish the ongoing need for the organization and how becoming a monthly partner gives us the confidence that we can depend on that money each month so we can focus on the crucial work before us.

Consider integrating your recurring giving program into all channels in onboarding, including:

Receipts are the first email and direct mail channel where we send proactive messages to donors. Receipts should be focused on affirming the donor. You can still include a passive mention of your recurring program and a link to learn more.

New-Donor Welcome Package to affirm the donor and their impact on the cause. This should include a passive mention of the sustainer program, at a minimum, up to a full call to action to join the program.

Sustainer Conversion Package is a piece focused on inspiring the new donor to see the kind of ongoing, lasting impact they can have. It shows them how a monthly commitment will help the organization focus on its core mission, reduce costs of fundraising, and give them the confidence to invest, knowing there is a group of faithful supporters standing with the organization. The package should include a straightforward sign-up process, a link to sign up online easily, and an option to mail in a voided check (EFT is ideal) or fill in a credit card.

Email onboarding should include a robust email welcome series early on in your new-donor experience, including both indirect and direct calls to action. Ensure emails are not entirely informational but include affirmation, relationship, and invitation.

Phone should be considered, though it is not always used in onboarding, especially since donors are often sensitive to how they will be treated by a nonprofit they've just given to. More testing is needed but consider a "no-strings-attached" thank-you call to affirm new donors. Later in the program, the phone is an effective channel that many of the most sophisticated nonprofits use to convert, upgrade, or reactivate donors.

TAKEAWAY: The best time for donors to convert from being new single-gift donors is in the first thirty to sixty days, starting at the point of the first gift. In this window, the donor's awareness and interest in the cause is at a high, and they have not yet settled into any pattern of giving.

After onboarding, there are several strategies that can be utilized throughout the year.

Always-On Conversion Strategies

Some elements can be put into place that are ongoing or evergreen. These include things like:

Receipt Inserts regularly, either bimonthly or quarterly, if you have other receipt inserts that you use.

Website Promotions/Online Donation Forms that promote and incentivize recurring giving conversion.

Secondary Calls to Action (CTAs) in existing communications such as direct mail appeals, newsletters, and emails.

Paid Search options to give on a recurring basis when people search for the organization or cause.

Digital Media to build audiences, capture names, and remarket of content and ads about recurring giving to people who have visited your website.

TAKEAWAY: In addition to onboarding, there are strategies that can be put into place to be always on—receipt inserts, website promotions, donation forms, secondary calls to action, paid search, and digital media.

In addition to always-on strategies, there should be active, specific conversion efforts several times throughout the year.

Punctuated Conversion Efforts

Throughout the year, there should be active times when you promote your subscription giving program and encourage donors to sign up.

These include the following:

Campaigns are dedicated multichannel efforts to create bumps in awareness and conversions for recurring giving. These campaigns typically feature a limited timeframe, clear goal, and a specific need across multiple channels.

Some of the most successful organizations I know that are converting donors to recurring at scale are using multichannel campaigns, particularly in the times of the year when there are lulls between campaigns.

Phone is a strong channel to invite existing donors to consider giving on a recurring basis. Like the campaigns, phone-based efforts should have a clear goal and specific reason and need for why you are inviting them to step up into a recurring relationship.

Direct mail recruitment-focused efforts are common, though sometimes they struggle to be cost-effective. Smart organizations tailor direct mail recruitment to donors who are new or have a demonstrated pattern of giving multiple gifts already to convert them to recurring.

Email can be used to regularly highlight recurring giving, in addition to emails utilized in campaigns. Consider telling stories of recurring donors as well as the impact of recurring giving on the cause.

Events are natural places where the organization has the full attention of donors and can invite them into recurring giving.

TAKEAWAY: On an ongoing basis, charities should have always-on activities that promote and position their sustainer program, complemented with punctuated campaigns and communications that create spikes of interest, awareness, and action.

Finally, let's look at how we care for recurring donors and cultivate relationships for the long term.

CHAPTER 28

Cultivate, Upgrade, Retain, Reactivate

MORE THAN 97 percent of the value of a subscription donor comes after the first recurring gift.

Let that sink in for a moment. A typical subscription donor's first gift represents *less than 3 percent* of what they will give over time. Because of this, the cultivation of recurring donors should be one of the most important priorities of your fundraising program.

More than 97 percent of the value of a subscription donor comes after the first recurring gift.

Once a recurring donor signs on, it is tempting to breathe a sigh of relief, send a receipt and an automated monthly email, and leave it there. Some nonprofit leaders even worry that if they communicate with donors, they will remind them of their ongoing giving and lose them.

This "set-it-and-forget-it" approach is an unfortunate tactic borrowed from low-value subscriptions with high churn. Consumers, just like today's donors, aren't fooled. Shaped by the subscription economy, they are savvy about tracking the subscriptions in their lives.

Effective subscription giving programs recognize the importance of ongoing cultivation from the beginning.

There are several stages throughout the life of a subscription donor. These include:

- Onboarding
- Cultivation
- Upgrading
- Retention
- Reactivation

In the spirit of getting our new subscription giving donors off to a good start, let's start with onboarding them.

Starting Off Right—Onboarding New Sustainers

A new subscription giving donor will give over thirty times the value of their first gift over the long term

A new subscription giving donor will give over thirty times the value of their first gift over the long term, so welcoming them well is essential for a long-term relationship.

A strong donor onboarding program acknowledges whether donors are new to the organization or were previously single-gift donors. It considers how to honor, affirm, and solidify care for the donors in the long term.

Treat your new recurring donors with authenticity and in a human way. One way to do that is to send communications from a specific individual—a real person they can respond to or call if needed. Often, this can be the development leader or the individual responsible for the program.

When designing (or redesigning) your new subscription giving donor onboarding experience, consider every element of the journey, including receipts, email, direct mail, phone, and mobile messaging.

When designing (or redesigning) your new subscription giving donor onboarding experience, consider every element of the journey

TAKEAWAY: More than 97 percent of the value of a recurring subscription donor comes after that first recurring gift. Keep that in mind as you craft a memorable welcome experience.

Once a donor is onboarded, you should cultivate the relationship continuously. Let's examine that next.

Stewarding the Relationship—Cultivating Sustainers

Organizations make two common mistakes regarding ongoing communication with recurring donors. First, they remove sustainers from ongoing communications, effectively sending them no communications at all. This is typically driven by a misguided assumption that recurring giving should be "set it and forget it."

The second mistake organizations make is not tailoring the existing donor experience, sending sustainers all existing communications, fundraising appeals, and so on.

Recurring donors are too valuable to leave in the dark or to be treated like everyone else. Remember, these donors are some of the most committed to your cause. They are also some of the most generous donors and are responsive to giving additional gifts throughout the year.

On an ongoing basis, subscription donors should receive a mix of affirmations, engagement, appeals, and newsletters. In some cases, recurring donors should also receive special extra-gift asks. Let's examine each in turn:

Affirmations mostly take the form of monthly updates on the progress gained thanks to the donor's faithfulness. Often, this takes the form of a receipt letter. Many—though not all—organizations mail their receipt letters, which ensures a high likelihood of being read and enables receipt inserts and other promotions to be included. The goal of these communications is to affirm the donor and help them see how their ongoing support is making an impact.

Engagement communications elicit a response or strengthen the relationship with the donor. These can include asking for feedback, responding to a question, inviting input, or inviting a donor to engage with content intended to deepen the relationship with the donor. Other ways to engage recurring donors include invitations to special events or town halls.

Appeals and newsletters serve as helpful informational touch points and are important given that recurring donors are often the most likely to respond to specific appeals. These are sent on a limited frequency, often as versions of existing appeals to single-gift donors, tailored to acknowledge the donor is a sustainer and making a case for the specific, urgent, one-time need. To determine which appeals to include, consider the most likely times and topics recurring donors would respond to. Newsletters tend to be more relational and engaging in content, so many organizations will send all newsletters to recurring donors.

Special extra-gift asks are tailored, timely, relevant, and specific asks of donors to give an additional gift. For example, organizations that offer child sponsorship will often send out an ask ahead of the sponsored child's birthday or the holidays and ask the donor to consider an extra gift to the program in honor of their sponsored child. This is based on the practice these organizations have to celebrate every child (no matter whether an extra gift is given), so it provides a natural place to ask a donor to help step in and give something extra for that child.

It is possible to see 25 percent or more extra giving from sustainers by cultivating them well.

By including donors in occasional regular appeals and tailoring special extra-gift asks to them, it is possible to see extra giving from sustainers in the 25 percent–plus range over and above their regular recurring giving.

As for what makes sense as an extra gift ask for your organization—consider your program. What times or types of projects would make sense to a donor to make a special ask for an extra gift? For example, if you are a social services nonprofit, there may be times of year when demand spikes. That could be an excellent time to tailor a special ask to recurring donors. Disasters or other unexpected needs are another time when it makes sense to donors that you might ask them to consider an extra gift.

TAKEAWAY: A well-designed ongoing cultivation program for recurring donors includes consistent affirmation, occasional asks, informational communications, engagement, and timely and relevant extra-gift asks.

Let's now look at increasing sustainer value through upgrades.

Increasing Value—Upgrading Sustainers

One of the most overlooked opportunities for charity subscription giving programs is increasing giving over the life of the recurring donor. Most nonprofits effectively hand the donor over to gift processing and leave it at that, not recognizing all they can do to care for, retain, and upgrade those donors.

In addition to extra single gifts, there are four ways for a subscription giving donor to upgrade their giving and increase long-term value.

- Upgrading Recurring Donation Amount
- Upgrading Payment Method
- Upgrading to Mid- or Major-Donor Level
- Upgrading to the Ultimate Gift—Legacy Giving

Upgrading Recurring Donation Amount

When asking donors to consider increasing their recurring gift amount, there are several channels and tactics, including phone, events, direct mail, and multichannel campaigns.

Phone is one of the best direct channels for upgrade asks. You can target donors who have not recently upgraded, are not very new, or exhibited some other behavior you don't want to call them.

Events are another great place for donors to increase their regular gifts. If you have an audience of existing recurring donors, it's an excellent opportunity to make the case and invite them to increase their regular giving.

Direct mail can be more expensive but has the benefit of being tangible and hard to ignore. If the piece is tailored to the need, urgency, and opportunity, direct mail can be a good place for donors to elect to increase their recurring giving.

Email is a less direct channel than the three we've covered so far, but it is also cheaper and benefits from being used much more frequently. For email, consider campaigns that incorporate multiple emails that invite recurring donors to increase their giving.

> Periodically offering ways for donors to increase their regular recurring gift amount is an effective way to increase commitment and donor value.

Multichannel campaigns can be used effectively to upgrade donors. In chapter 27, we talked about utilizing multichannel campaigns to convert existing donors to subscription giving. Those same campaigns can be modified to include existing recurring donors with an upgrade message.

When asking donors to consider increasing their regular giving amount, there should be a good reason. Those reasons include increased need, expanding scope, or some special limited-time opportunity that the charity can only take advantage of with increased donor support.

TAKEAWAY: Periodically offering ways for donors to increase their regular recurring gift amount is an effective way to increase commitment and donor value. Just ensure you include a reason for asking for an increased commitment.

Upgrading Payment Method

An often overlooked aspect of increasing giving over time is when donors change to a more advantageous payment method. In the United States, most recurring giving is done via credit card, but EFT/ACH giving is the most desirable, with double-digit higher retention rates. EFT giving also has lower costs and fees associated with it.

Approximately 25 percent of credit card transactions churn annually due to issues with payment processing, expiration dates changing, and cards getting replaced. So, a change in payment method to a more reliable method, such as from credit card to EFT, is indeed an upgrade.

Ideally, charities encourage donors to start with EFT/ACH. Let the donor do what they will, but at least make them aware that the preferred payment method is EFT/ACH.

After sign-up, charities can occasionally invite donors to switch their method to EFT. Explain the benefits to the donor—reliability, avoiding the hassle of credit cards, lower costs, and more impact. This can be done through receipt inserts, phone calls, or email campaigns.

Alternatively, an increasingly popular tactic enables donors to elect to cover processing fees via a checkbox when signing up to ensure 100 percent of the gift goes to the charity. This option is not without controversy, as it does add some friction to the donation process. Yet, depending on the platform, 50–65 percent of the time, donors elected to cover fees when asked to do so, according to Claire Axelrad, chief fundraising coach at Bloomerang and principal at Clarification.[41]

TAKEAWAY: Some payment methods, like EFT/ACH, are better than others with regard to lower processing costs and churn. When a donor elects to use EFT/ACH or to switch to that payment type, they are in effect, upgrading their giving to the organization.

Upgrading to Mid- or Major-Donor Level

Recurring donors are typically the most loyal and the most invested in your cause, so it logically follows that they may be prospects for significant gifts.

Consider that a $500 annual donor works out to less than $42/mo. You may not think of a $42 donor as a significant donor, but you would think of a donor who gives $500 in a year worth paying attention to. Likewise, a $1,000 donor is just $83/month. It shifts one's perspective when you think about it that way.

Remember: subscription giving is all about long-term value, including being strategic about identifying and cultivating potential mid- and major-level donors.

To prospect for midlevel and major donors, consider a threshold for additional treatment when onboarding new recurring donors. Consider a wealth screening process for all new recurring donors. You may have a volunteer call to thank all new sustainers under a certain amount, but the director executive or donor rep calls those above a certain threshold.

You may send additional emails from an individual. You might assign them a representative dedicated to cultivating relationships with donors.

Some potential major donors will give a test gift of a smaller amount to see how the organization treats them. You never know when a potential large donor is giving you a smaller amount, and how you treat them may lead to a deeper relationship.

TAKEAWAY: It's important to be intentional with your recurring donors—midlevel and major donors are in your recurring giving program. Are you looking for them and giving them opportunities to engage more deeply?

Let's now look at the ultimate upgrade—legacy giving.

Upgrading to the Ultimate Gift—Legacy Giving

One of the greatest sources of planned gifts comes from recurring donors. Recurring donors are six times more likely to leave an organization in their will or make a legacy gift to an organization.

> Recurring donors are six times more likely to leave an organization in their will or make a legacy gift to an organization.

Legacy giving researcher Dr. Claire Routely says, "The leading factor that will determine whether someone will make a planned gift to your organization is their level of loyalty."[42]

It makes sense that your most loyal donors would also be more likely to give the most significant gifts of their lives—either via their will or estate or through some other legacy gift after the sale of a business.

If some of the best candidates for estate and other planned gifts are your recurring donors, what are some strategies you can use?

- **Talk about It**—Share about planned and legacy giving in your communications with donors.
- **Tell Stories**—According to Russell James, a professor and researcher specializing in planned giving, donors are motivated by values and stories rather than taxes or benefits.
- **Invite Stories**—The more you allow donors to reflect on why your cause is important to them, the more you invite them to connect their identity with the cause.
- **Donor Surveys**—Surveys invite donor feedback, enabling donors to indicate interest in leaving a legacy with the cause.

TAKEAWAY: Recurring donors are six times more likely than single-gift donors to give a legacy or planned gift, but unless they know, they are less likely to act. Talk about it in communications, tell stories, and invite the donors to share their stories.

After upgrading donors, we need to look at retaining them next.

Keeping Them—Retaining Sustainers

In the business world, it's widely understood that keeping existing customers is less expensive than getting new ones. The same goes for nonprofits and fundraising—keeping existing donors is less costly and more valuable than getting new ones.

Since more than 97 percent of the value of recurring donors is in their long-term giving, keeping those donors to the best of our ability is critical.

There are two ways nonprofits lose recurring donors:

1. **Voluntary Churn**—When a donor intentionally chooses to stop giving on a recurring basis.
2. **Involuntary Churn**—When a donor stops giving unintentionally due to an issue such as payment failure.

Let's explore when each type of churn occurs and how nonprofit leaders can reduce that churn.

Preventing Voluntary Churn

There are two stages in which we can impact voluntary churn—when a donor is considering stopping giving (lapse prevention) and when they decide to stop giving and act.

There are two ways nonprofits lose recurring donors—voluntary churn and involuntary churn.

In the category of lapse prevention, the first step is to determine if there are key times when recurring donors lapse. These can vary depending on your organization, donors, and the nature of your recurring giving program. For example, in the world of child sponsorship, it's not uncommon for there to be an increase in churn anytime a donor's sponsored child leaves the program, necessitating a new sponsored child to be introduced to the donor.

Are there natural windows for your charity for recurring donors to voluntarily stop giving? Other examples might be at the two or three-month mark after signing up or just before the first anniversary of giving. The key is looking at your data to determine if there are common points when recurring donors lapse.

Once you have a sense of the most common times and situations when donors stop giving, consider ways to address churn during those windows, ideally proactively. Is there a weak point in your experience that you can turn into a strength? See chapter 21 about elevating peaks and flipping pits.

What you do to prevent churn depends highly on the context of your program, but some things you might look at include:

Communicate proactively ahead of time to address the reasons for the potential churn. Test different messages or activities that might shift the donor's perspective and decision to stop giving.

Automate processes to minimize disruption. In the example of child sponsorship, if you see heightened churn when asking donors to choose their next sponsored child, consider auto-assigning the next available child and allowing donors to change the selection if they would like.

Enhance the experience by improving upon whatever factors lead the donor to stop giving. Sometimes, something needs to be changed in how donors are recruited in the initial sign-up period—for example, you may have intentionally or unintentionally set expectations about the duration or type of experience that results in undesirable churn.

Leverage data to better predict and target donors most likely to churn. There are a number of data models out there from different CRM, agency, and technology providers that attempt to use data and behavior to predict when donors are most likely to lapse. Consider testing some of these models and proactively changing your treatment of these donors to see if you can reduce churn.

No matter what you do, some donors will stop giving on a recurring basis. This is not always a bad thing, so whatever you do, don't feel like you are failing if you lose 5–15 percent of your recurring donors each year.

TAKEAWAY: Voluntary churn can be proactively reduced by identifying key drop-off points or behaviors that lead to canceling recurring giving and seeking to address the root causes of that churn.

The other area where voluntary churn can be prevented is at the point of cancellation.

Voluntary Churn at the Point of Cancellation

When donors do express a desire to cancel, there are a few things that the organization can do.

Acknowledge and affirm the donor. Show empathy and appreciation, and seek to understand why they want to cancel their ongoing giving—"I'm sorry to hear that. We want to thank you and affirm the difference you've made [in your cause] over the [time period]. If you don't mind, can I ask why you are calling to cancel your giving?"

Offer pause/skip or downgrade. A retained donor is more valuable than a lapsed donor, so depending on the reason given, consider offering ways for the donor to stay involved at a lower giving level or by skipping for some number of months if the cancelation is due to temporary circumstances.

You might say, "You may already be aware of this, but we've heard from donors who care about the cause but aren't able to give right now. If you are interested, we can pause your donation for [period of time]. Would you like to do that?"

Ask and learn. Regardless of whether the donor decides to stay or not, capture the reason why. Ideally, capture both verbatim responses and code the reason into three to six buckets (e.g., financial hardship, issue with the organization, no longer interested in giving) so you can understand the most common reasons for cancellation.

Don't make it hard. Treating donors well is the right thing to do and engenders more goodwill than any lost revenue you might experience by making it difficult to cancel. At a minimum, include a clear phone number (that someone will answer) where donors can cancel, update payment or other information, or change their gift amount.

TAKEAWAY: The point at which the donor chooses to cancel is another space where you can learn and potentially retain the donor. The goal is a positive experience with your organization by affirming them, offering alternatives, and seeking to learn.

The next area where you can make the most significant impact is preventing the unnecessary loss of recurring donors—involuntary churn.

Preventing Involuntary Churn

While data is relatively limited on involuntary churn in the charitable giving sector, according to the subscription management platform Recurly, approximately 53 percent of all customer attrition falls under involuntary churn, making it a significant issue for subscription businesses. For donors who are typically more loyal than subscribers, the percentage of churn due to involuntary factors would be more than 53 percent.

Technical issues with payments are the largest source of involuntary churn in recurring giving programs—payment information changes on the donor's end or a transition in payment processors or donation providers at the charity.

There are several ways to prevent or respond to involuntary churn.

Conversion to a more stable giving payment type (EFT). We discussed this earlier in this chapter, but one significant way to prevent involuntary churn is to get donors to sign up for or convert to a more stable payment type like EFT.

Credit and debit card auto-updaters. Donation processors have different capabilities for auto-updating expired or replaced cards. Ensure that your donation processor can automatically update expiration dates and even process replacement cards in some circumstances.

Retry failed payments. Sometimes, a payment will fail for reasons other than an expired or replaced card–due to technical issues, insufficient funds, or otherwise. It's essential to have a process to retry failed payments automatically. Ideally, you should be able to have your processor retry payment a certain number of retries at different times.

Automated messages to donors. If the automated retry and replacement methods fail, ensure there is an automatic way to contact donors and ask them to provide updated payment information. This should happen in a timely manner.

For example, I'm a monthly donor to International Justice Mission. When they could not process a recurring donation payment, they sent a very clear, kindly worded email letting me know, including a link to update payment information with my user name and offering a direct phone number for their Giving Team should I want to speak with someone.

Conduct outreach for failed payments. Some donors will not see or respond to automated emails. After a couple of emails, there should be a process of direct outreach to donors.

Personal phone calls and emails (from a human). Automated emails are easy to miss, but a more personal email from a person is more likely to (1) be delivered and (2) be noticed by the donor.

Send direct mail. Direct mail has the advantage of being a channel that gets many donors' attention. It's worth it as a way to get donors' attention who have missed other alerts, whether a simple postcard or a short letter with a clear process to update payment information.

If possible, send a text. A more advanced option would be an automated text with a secure link to update payment information, but this is dependent on your tech stack.

Offer the ability to update payment information online. Ideally, donors can update their payment information online, whether through a secure page where they can enter new payment information or a full-fledged system where they can manage their accounts.

TAKEAWAY: Involuntary churn is the most significant source of lost donors for most organizations. Fortunately, several preventative measures can be taken to improve churn in both the back-end technology and the donor experience.

However, sometimes, donors are lost due to involuntary churn. In these cases, it's important to flag your donor records.

Tracking Lapsed Recurring Donors

It is essential to have a process for knowing in your donor CRM when a recurring donor has lapsed or canceled their giving. Some nonprofits make the mistake of not flagging or being able to tell when a recurring donor has stopped giving.

Even if a donor lapses without payment, you should have a rule for when you consider them lapsed and mark them as such. That might be six months, three months, or another window that makes sense for your organization.

Updating data records is vital for two reasons. First, we need to understand how our program is doing and not be inflated with donors who have lapsed or canceled. Second, knowing who has lapsed or canceled is critical to reactivation—the next area we will review together.

When donors lapse, assuming these are permanent decisions is a mistake.

Let's turn to the final component of a healthy recurring giving program—the reactivation of lapsed recurring donors.

Lapsed Recurring Donor Reactivation

Every nonprofit has a growing list of subscription giving donors who are no longer active. The nature of donor churn means that more people are added to the list of former recurring donors each year.

There are many reasons why a recurring donor stops giving—financial hardship, losing touch with the cause, changing giving priorities, and so on. Often, it's the result of some simple circumstance, such as a new credit card being issued or a change of address that never gets updated.

When donors lapse, assuming these are permanent decisions is a mistake. Sometimes, in the case of involuntary churn, the donor is unaware that they are no longer giving to you on a recurring basis.

When reactivating lapsed recurring donors, the first place to start is with your existing acquisition and conversion strategies.

Reactivation Using Existing Efforts

The first place to reactivate lapsed subscription giving donors is by incorporating them into any existing sustainer acquisition or conversion efforts.

Depending on how large your list is, consider segmenting your lapsed recurring by recently lapsed (less than twelve months), twelve to twenty-four months lapsed, and twenty-five-plus months lapsed (or similar)—there are different types of messaging and treatments you might give these different groups.

Consider the following strategies for reactivation as you communicate to this segment of donors:

Multichannel Campaigns—In sustainer recruitment efforts, include lapsed subscription donors in micro campaigns with customized messaging acknowledging their support in the past and stating why their renewed support is needed now.

Phone—Phone is a great channel for a personal conversation with a donor. You can acknowledge their previous support, make a case for renewed support, and ask them to consider renewing their sustained giving.

Email—Email is the workhorse of lapsed sustainer reactivation—a recent campaign with a client saw nearly 10 percent of signups for recurring giving from previously lapsed sustainers. Include lapsed recurring donors in conversion communications, again ideally with variable messaging acknowledging past support and inviting them to renew.

Direct Mail—Direct mail can be leveraged to reactivate recurring donors, either via a modified version of a recurring giving recruitment package or a postcard or handwritten card, thanking the donor for their past, ongoing support, making the case for the present need, and asking them if they would be willing to renew their giving.

All other marketing channels, such as social media, search, events, your website, digital media, and so on, can help reactivate sustainers.

TAKEAWAY: The first and most efficient way to reactivate lapsed recurring donors is to include them strategically in your acquisition and conversion efforts. You are already doing the work to execute these strategies, so they can pull double duty for a limited amount of additional effort.

TAKEAWAY: If you don't employ all channels for acquisition and conversion, it can be a good idea to leverage one or more of these channels to invite lapsed sustainers to renew.

We've just covered a lot—let's recap as we conclude part 3—Designing and Managing a Thriving Sustainer Program.

Recap—Cultivate, Upgrade, Retain, Reactivate

More than 97 percent of the value of recurring donors occurs after the first recurring gift, so optimizing the experience for growth is essential.

The recurring donor experience begins with a solid onboarding and ongoing cultivation strategy—one that is tailored to them. It includes periodic and relevant invitations to increase their commitment and proactively retain them. Finally, it invites recurring donors who lapse to reactivate their support.

Over the course of part 3, we've covered the essential steps in building a thriving recurring giving program:

- Identifying Your Stage of Maturity—Structuring for Success
- Understanding Where You Are—Measurement
- Go On Your Donor's Journey—Mapping the Experience
- Talk to Donors—Human-Centered Design
- Nail Your Offer—Ongoing-Value Proposition
- Justifying Ongoing Involvement—Crafting an Offer
- Design and Launch (or Relaunch)—Program Design
- Get Your Tech Stack Right—Systems and Platforms
- Grow Your Program—Recruit Everywhere
- Cultivate, Upgrade, Retain, Reactivate

As you consider the strategies we've covered in part 3, refer back to the impact-effort matrix from chapter 18. This tool is a meaningful way to prioritize your efforts.

In part 4, we'll conclude by looking ahead to the trends continuing to shape the landscape of subscription giving and predicting how it will continue to evolve.

Let's do that now!

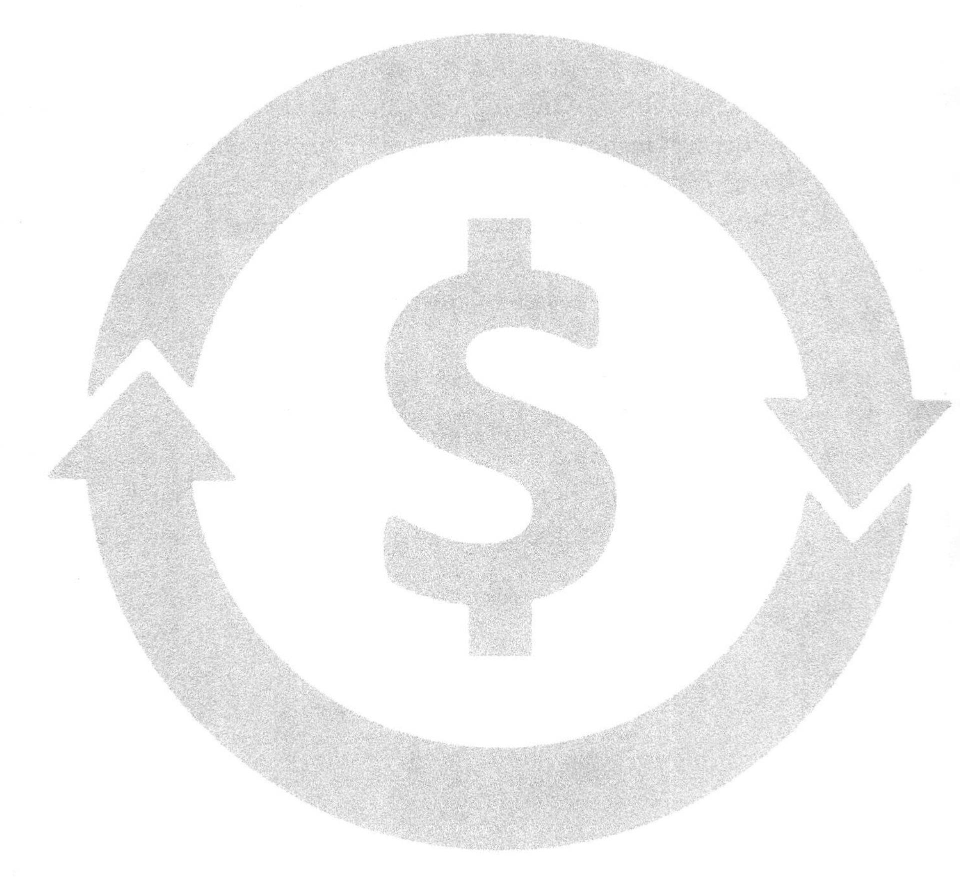

PART 4

The Future of Sustainable Giving

CHAPTER 29

Predictions on the Future of Sustainable Giving

IF YOU'VE MADE it this far, you care about how recurring giving is changing. In these final few chapters, let's look at predictions for where subscription giving is headed.

The future of sustainable giving is bright.

Momentum is building.

There are five areas where I expect to see continued evolution and breakthrough innovation over the next few years.

1. Organizational Maturity
2. Technological Advancement
3. AI-Enhanced Capability
4. Financial Innovation
5. Donor Experience

> The future of sustainable giving is bright.

Let's start by looking at how organizations will mature in their approach to subscription giving.

Predictions: Organizational Maturity

Organizations will develop a more sophisticated understanding of and approach to recurring giving.

As charities seek to build thriving subscription giving programs, several areas—internal structure, resourcing, data architecture, measurement and reporting, and financial models—will need to mature rapidly in the coming years.

Prediction: Organizations Will Adopt a Sustainer-First Mindset

Increasingly, charities will prioritize recurring giving as a central pillar of their mass fundraising efforts. We discussed this already starting to happen in chapter 15 with charities like charity: water.

Increasingly, charities will prioritize recurring giving as a central pillar of their mass fundraising efforts.

It will be unmistakable to donors and prospects who the core of the support base is—those faithful, recurring supporters who provide stable, ongoing support to make the mission possible and enable the organization to boldly make plans, knowing they have a growing, loyal base of supporters.

Internally, the organization will see its sustainer program as the core of the donor file, and planning will always ask the question: How will this add to or subtract from our central source of recurring revenue funding?

Prediction: Resources Will Be Dedicated to Subscription Giving

Resources—time, money, personnel—will be dedicated to growing subscription giving in increasing amounts.

Charities will elevate subscription giving as a core income program, on the level with major donor or single-gift programs. This will lead to the creation of integrated subscription giving teams responsible for the holistic growth of the recurring giving programs.

These dedicated personnel will have dedicated budgets—budgets that will grow as charities see the powerful compounding effect of investing in sustainable recurring revenue. As they resource the program, they will see the fruits of dedicating resources to growing and enhancing it—monthly recurring revenue grows, churn decreases, reactivation improves, and more dollars go to the cause.

As organizations evolve from no one responsible, to shared responsibility, to a single individual responsible, to a dedicated team, they will see the fruits of that increased focus.

Prediction: Data and Reporting Will Be Fully Subscription Ready

At most nonprofits today, measurement and reporting are optimized to drive single gifts. This single-gift mindset is a barrier to growing recurring giving because it results in misaligned incentives and a lack of clarity on how subscription giving programs are performing.

In the future, dashboards and key measurements from the subscription economy will be commonplace. Metrics such as monthly recurring revenue (MRR), annual recurring revenue (ARR), involuntary churn, voluntary churn, and projected long-term value, will become commonplace, and charities will use the insights to grow their programs.

Additionally, data structures and data hygiene will improve. Out-of-date or bad data prevents many organizations from understanding and acting on the opportunities and looming problems within their programs. It also inhibits the organization's ability to truly personalize and treat the donor as if it knows them.

Prediction: Financial Planning Will Incorporate Subscription Giving

How organizations plan for, budget, and evaluate fundraising in the era of sustainable giving will evolve.

In a single-gift paradigm, all financial planning is based on the *present and past value*—how much did we spend, and what value did that generate? Any consideration of the future is limited from a financial perspective.

> In the future, dashboards and key measurements from the subscription economy will be commonplace.

Short-term financial planning leads to shortsighted focus—hitting this year's numbers and getting a certain number of donors in the door this year at the expense of long-term value and returns.

In a sustainer-centric paradigm, financial planning is based on the *present and future value*. Organizations will think of their sustainer program as an asset that produces ongoing recurring revenue for years to come.

There are a couple of advantages to this mindset. First, organizations recognize that upfront investment leads to significant margins. Once a sustaining donor is onboard, the cost to maintain that relationship is a fraction of the cost of cultivating and keeping a single-gift donor. And second, with such high retention rates, the program can snowball positively. With a growing sustainer program, each year, the organization starts with a larger base than the year before and builds on the snowball from there.

> In a sustainer-centric paradigm, financial planning is based on the *present and future value.*

But this requires a paradigm shift. Financial planning needs to focus on generating value, not just for the next twelve months but for the next sixty months and beyond. It must account for the high retention rates associated with recurring giving. It also needs to account for the "churn and burn" that single-gift programs are based on. In a single-gift program, it's not uncommon to churn more than 75 percent of the new donors acquired each year. With such a leaky bucket, tons of emphasis is put on acquiring new donors, knowing that three-quarters or more of them will not give again in the next year.

However, with subscription giving, the numbers flip—75 percent of recurring donors typically stick around. Fewer donors are needed, because they stick around and are of higher value. Once the snowball has grown, it creates powerful momentum that is wonderful. It takes a new financial mindset to get there.

TAKEAWAY: As organizations mature in their approach to subscription giving, they increasingly adopt a sustainer-first mindset, dedicating staff and budget to growing the

> program, improving measurement and data tracking, and how they do financial planning.

Next, let's explore how the technology available to charities will increasingly become sustainer first.

CHAPTER 30

Technological Advancement

MOST TECHNOLOGY TODAY was built in a world before the subscription economy and certainly before the subsequent rise of recurring subscription giving.

Because many of these trends are new over the past decade, subscription giving is not baked into the core of most fundraising tools today.

Over the coming years, technology will increasingly incorporate subscription giving principles and approaches. At the same time, new technologies and products will come online with subscription giving built in at their core.

> Technology will increasingly incorporate subscription giving principles and approaches.

At the same time, the consumer world, subscriptions, and the financial sector will continue to evolve, bringing new capabilities to consumers, subscription businesses, and technology companies.

Let's examine three specific areas where technology will advance.

Prediction: Technology Products and Services Will Become Sustainer First

The technologies and products that power subscription giving will evolve up and down the tech stack. New companies and products that are sustainer first and purpose-built for fundraising in the subscription economy will rise. Other existing technologies will see the value of subscription giving and retool to incorporate recurring giving as a core feature of their products.

This sustainer-first evolution will take place across several areas within technology providers:

Data Architecture—The type and structure of data in many technology platforms actively inhibits and works against subscription giving. For example, in some platforms, if a donor stops giving on a recurring basis, it's as if they never were a recurring donor, making reactivation efforts impossible. Sustainer-first technologies will be built on a modern data architecture that accounts for the centrality of recurring giving.

Customer Experience—Donors are shaped by their interactions and expectations with the best companies in the subscription economy, from Netflix to Amazon Prime. Sustainer-first technologies will incorporate features and functionalities that subscription-conditioned donors expect, such as the ability to pause giving, update payment information, view reporting, and the like.

Automation—Sustainer-first technologies will enable the myriad use cases for automation, from administrative functions like payment recovery processes to proactive, personalized, and triggered communications. The future is more about creating an operating system of automation and triggers. Any donor can enter at any time, and their behavior and information should trigger an automated, personalized donor experience.

Reporting—Built-in reporting will be subscription giving–centric for sustainer-first technologies. It will no longer require special customization, manual data processing, and custom visualizations to understand the performance of a subscription giving sustainer program. Sustainer-first technology will be built from the ground up to surface the data and insights necessary to take advantage of opportunities and identify problems before they emerge.

AI-Driven Capabilities—We'll discuss this further in the next chapter, but sustainer-first technologies will incorporate machine learning techniques and features that enable proactive and automated treatments. AI-driven features will become commonplace, including churn prediction and prevention, transaction payment recovery, personalization of asks, communications, and experiences, as well as triggered communications based on patterns in the data.

Prediction: The Rise of Alternative Payment Methods (Digital Wallets)

There used to be three payment options for donations: check, credit card, and EFT/ACH. But over the past several years, we've seen the rise of digital wallets and peer-to-peer payment systems.

A digital wallet is "an electronic device, online service, or software program that allows one party to make electronic transactions with another party."[43] Examples of digital wallets include PayPal, an online payment provider and a bank; mobile app payment platforms like Apple Pay and Google Pay, and peer-to-peer apps like Venmo and Cash App.

The past several years, we've seen the rise of digital wallets and peer-to-peer payment systems.

eMarketer found that nearly two-thirds of smartphone users would use mobile wallets by the end of 2024, up from half in 2023. In 2023, eMarketer found that the most popular form of digital wallet was PayPal, with 36 percent of US adults using the platform for online purchases. Apple Pay was the next most common (18%), followed by Venmo (15%), Google Wallet (9%), and Samsung Pay (5%).[44]

Whatever the payment method, it's clear that the types of accepted payment donors will want in the future will grow. In the near term, nonprofit leaders should watch the consumer space to see which digital wallet payment types rise to the top.

Prediction: Subscription Economy Tech and Consumer Preferences Will Evolve

The world of subscriptions, subscription businesses, and the financial sector will continue to evolve, bringing new capabilities and preferences.

This will include improved technology for handling payments and involuntary churn, significantly reducing the unusually high and unnecessary churn due to failed payment processes.

There are other ways that subscriptions will continue to evolve and shape technology. For example, subscribers expect to be able to see and manage their entire relationship in one interface. Donors will expect to be able to access information about their giving subscriptions and to be treated accordingly.

TAKEAWAY: The technology that supports and enables subscription giving is a few years behind the rise of the subscription economy. Over the coming years, a class of sustainer-first technologies will be developed, removing the worst limitations and enabling enhanced recurring donor experiences and growth.

Next, let's go one step further and look at the impact of one set of technologies on the landscape of recurring giving—Artificial Intelligence.

CHAPTER 31
AI-Driven Capabilities and Experiences

ARTIFICIAL INTELLIGENCE HAS been the most hyped advancement of the past decade, and for good reason—it's impacted nearly every area of life and promises to transform the world in ways we can barely imagine.

In marketing and fundraising, AI is not new. It's been used for decades in the form of machine learning. But with the emergence of generative AI and large language models (LLMs), we are on the verge of an entirely new set of advancements.

Briefly, generative AI refers to deep-learning models that can generate high-quality text, images, and other content based on the data they were trained on. Large language models, or LLMs, are a specialized type of generative artificial intelligence trained on vast amounts of text to understand existing content and generate human-like content.

The most helpful way I've found to think about AI is as a coworker.

AI as a Coworker

Throughout history, technology has primarily served as a *power tool*—augmenting human ability and intelligence. We've invented machines that help us build skyscrapers, plant crops, do complex mathematical calculations, fly to space, and so on. But at the end of the day, all that technology was helping humans do what they do, just better and faster.

Artificial intelligence is different. It can do things that no human can do and at a scale that no human could achieve. In this way, artificial intelligence is less like a power tool and more like a colleague—a *coworker* with gifts and abilities that you and I don't have. So, in the twenty-first century, technology has begun to act more like a coworker.

In the twenty-first century, technology has begun to act more like a coworker.

Over the coming years, as we learn to work better with this coworker called AI, there are several areas that will impact subscription giving.

TAKEAWAY: Technology has historically acted as a power tool—empowering humans to do more of what we can do. Artificial intelligence is different—it acts as a coworker, bringing different skills and capabilities with which we can collaborate.

AI will enable capabilities and experiences that were not previously possible at scale.

Prediction: AI Enabled Targeting and Segmentation Will Help Find New Audiences and Communicate with Existing Ones

Artificial intelligence tools will increasingly help us identify and send the right messages to the right people at the right time and in the right channel. Today, segmentation is still relatively rudimentary, determining who to send messages to in large groupings.

The future will see increasingly one-to-one decisions, where messages will be automated and tailored to the individual level based on the donor or prospect.

In other words, AI will enable the precise execution of the vision for marketing:

> The *right message*
> To the *right person*
> At the *right time*
> In the *right channel*

AI-based targeting and segmentation tools, such as lookalike audiences, will increasingly be used to identify and target audiences most likely to respond.

Prediction: Predictive Modeling Will Be Used to Encourage Outcomes

If targeting and segmentation determine who should receive a particular communication or campaign, then predictive modeling is about projecting likely behavior.

Models will be increasingly used to predict behavior and trigger proactive and automated experiences. Some examples include the following:

- An AI-based model can predict when a subscription giving donor is most likely to lapse. Charities can then be proactive in preventing donors from lapsing.
- An AI model predicts when individual donors would most likely increase their recurring amount, triggering a specialized communication treatment inviting them to do so.
- An AI model predicts that a specific single-gift donor will likely convert to recurring in March–June, and that a particular channel, such as phone, is likely most effective for this donor. Even though the nonprofit doesn't have a campaign happening in that timeframe, a phone call outreach is triggered for this particular donor, with accompanying emails.

This brings us to the next area where AI will transform recurring donors—automation.

Prediction: Automation and Streamlining of Operations, Data, Processes, and Overhead

AI tools will empower deeper automation of the donor experience and streamlining of operations to run an effective and powerful recurring giving program.

One of the promises of subscription recurring giving is that the program can scale revenue without scaling expenses. With a subscription, the cost to add one more customer is tiny compared to the upfront cost of building the subscription. Likewise, for subscription giving, the cost to add a recurring donor is small, making each incremental new sustainer easier and cheaper.

Nonprofit subscription giving programs will leverage AI to grow programs and scale without significant overhead.

This will impact both the front-end donor experience and back-end operations. The front-end donor experience will benefit from automation and triggered communications and treatments based on donor behavior, life stage, and other modeled attributes. And back-end operations will benefit from simple automation of tasks, data processing, report building, and so on.

> Models will be increasingly used to predict behavior and trigger proactive and automated experiences.

The final area where AI will transform subscription giving is the donor experience.

Prediction: The Donor Experience Will Be Enhanced via Communications and Personalization

Beyond automation and triggered communications, AI will make possible a level of personalization and creative expression tailored to individuals that has historically been too time-consuming and too costly to be practical.

Imagine utilizing AI to customize an onboarding series based on the kinds of content a new subscription giving donor consumed in the weeks leading up to becoming a donor.

Imagine tailoring a story of affirmation to a donor, incorporating them into the story based on how long they've been giving, what they've given to, and how they came into the organization. The possibilities for personalizing the donor experience are endless.

TAKEAWAY: AI will enhance charities' ability to target the right people at the right time with the right message and create great experiences, encouraging desired behaviors, automation of operations, and improving the donor experience.

Let's first look at how targeting and segmentation will continue to improve thanks to AI.

CHAPTER 32
Financial Innovation

NEW AND UNIQUELY valuable financial strategies and models will emerge from the subscription economy that will shape subscription giving.

These financial models will prove innovative for charities and help them grow recurring revenue.

The first is that some nonprofits will experiment with paid subscriptions.

Prediction: Charities Will Increasingly Experiment with Paid Subscriptions That Provide Ongoing Value

Particularly for charities that provide a benefit to donors as beneficiaries, some nonprofits will develop and refine paid subscriptions that prove to be valuable to donors.

These paid subscriptions look more like traditional subscriptions with a clear value proposition and might be for any number of things—goods, services, content, training, access, community, and so on.

The common denominator is that individuals or organizations would be willing to pay on an ongoing basis in exchange for value. The charitable component is less pronounced, although subscribing to a product or service from a cause likely has altruistic value.

> Some nonprofits will develop and refine paid subscriptions that prove to be valuable to donors.

Prediction: Autopay and Unique Financial Payment Methods

One unique approach we see increasingly is organizations leveraging autopay for gift types beyond the donor's regular recurring gift.

The most relevant example is organizations asking donors to automate an extra gift annually. For organizations where the additional gift is related to a predictable need that occurs each year, charities are increasingly inviting donors to set that up to happen each year automatically. For example, if the extra gift is for an annual event such as a sponsored child's birthday or a holiday outreach, then it is natural for the charity to offer the donor an option to set up that extra gift to happen each year at the same time.

We will also see other unique financial payments arise as digital wallet technologies mature. Examples include:

- **Mobile App Store Recurring Payments:** Many mobile apps incorporate recurring subscription payments, which a charity might leverage for subscription or giving purposes.
- **Easy Mobile Wallet Payments:** For example, at some point, it will be common to tap on a link in a text message to trigger

an easy Apple, Google, or Samsung Pay prompt, enabling the donor to give in two or three taps.

- **Tap to Pay:** Increasingly, the combination of physical NFC (near field communication) chips and mobile payment technologies will make it super easy to give a donation at a store checkout, sitting in the pew at a church, or at a local charity 5k or volunteer packing event. A simple tap and click, and the donor has given.

The next trend we will continue to see is donors choosing to give recurring gifts via donor-advised funds.

Prediction: Recurring Giving via Donor-Advised Funds

Giving via donor-advised funds (DAFs) has been growing over the past several years, driven by several factors, including tax advantages, anonymity and privacy, legacy planning, investment growth, and more. According to the National Philanthropic Trust, the *2023 Donor-Advised Fund* report found that giving from DAFs amounted to $52 billion in 2022 from nearly two million donor accounts.[45]

Reviewing the report mentioned prior, NonProfit PRO pointed out that donations from donor-advised funds are increasing on a recurring, regular basis. Fidelity Charitable reported that 31 percent of their gifts were scheduled repeat gifts, "showing loyalty to a nonprofit and an emerging type of recurring donor."

> 31 percent of DAF gifts were scheduled repeat gifts, "showing loyalty to a nonprofit and an emerging type of recurring donor."

The trend of recurring giving via DAFs is more than just isolated to one financial institution—Schwab Charitable reported that fully 35 percent of their grants were recurring gifts.

While DAF gifts can be a challenge to attribute, understanding that donors are increasingly giving on a recurring basis via donor-advised funds signals that charities should consider strategically promoting that type of giving to donors.

Prediction: Utilizing Corporate Partnerships to Grow Recurring Revenue

In chapter 27, we discussed the opportunity to use matching gifts to drive the acquisition and conversion of recurring donors. One form of match is where employees can apply for and receive corporate matching gifts from their employers for recurring giving. This is one of the opportunities that will continue to exist for donors and corporations, and charities have a role in encouraging companies to offer matching gifts and communicating with donors to ensure they are aware of the opportunity.

Beyond corporate matching, there are other opportunities in corporate relationships—specifically, cause marketing around consumer subscriptions and comarketing opportunities.

Cause marketing enables companies to align with causes. There are opportunities to become a charity of choice for subscription-based companies and donate a portion of their proceeds.

For example, KiwiCo is known for educational subscription boxes for kids. Its philanthropic arm aligns with various educational and environmental causes. In the past, KiwiCo has donated to foster kids in partnership with the Ticket to Dream Foundation and offered a "Buy One, Give One" program with Toys for Tots, in which every purchase of a KiwiCo box resulted in an educational toy crate donated for each crate purchased. More than twenty thousand KiwiCo activity and toy crates were donated to children in need.[46]

Comarketing opportunities also exist, aligning companies with causes to drive awareness for the cause and providing a mutual benefit—the charity gets awareness and a way to acquire names and donors. In exchange, the company gets to be aligned with the cause and drives its business objectives.

A historical example of comarketing has been at the store checkout. In the subscription economy, especially with tap-to-pay solutions, I expect to see efforts aimed at ongoing subscription donor acquisition via tap-to-pay.

Prediction: Growth Will Increasingly Be Funded in Unique Ways

The final category to watch is financial models that enable charities to increase their investment in growing recurring giving programs.

One of the significant challenges to scaling sustainer programs is the time it takes to pay back the initial cost of acquiring the donor. Typically, the payback period can be twelve to eighteen months from the initial recurring gift to breakeven. In the long term, this is well worth it—in 2024, Neon One found that recurring donors give for an average of 7.7 years. That translates to the vast majority of recurring gifts going straight to impact with little overhead.

> Innovative financial models will increasingly play a role in funding the growth of subscription giving.

Since it takes twelve to eighteen months to break even on the cost of a subscription giving donor, cash flow becomes an issue.

Innovative financial models will increasingly play a role in funding the growth of subscription giving. These unique financial funding mechanisms include:

Foundation Grants: Some organizations have associated foundations and can appeal for grants specifically for investing in capacity building.

Investments from Cash Reserves: Some organizations have substantial cash reserves, which allow them to finance growth with specific agreements about payback periods.

Investments from Excess Capital: There are different circumstances where a charity might see an infusion of capital—the sale of a building for example, or an undesignated estate gift. Whatever the source of the funds, these can be investment opportunities.

Buy Now, Pay Later: If you've ever received a new phone from your carrier and paid it off over two years, you've used Buy Now, Pay Later, or BNPL. Businesses offer this because they can access all of the funds from your purchase upfront via the financial provider, even though you are paying over time. BNPL providers make their money through interest on those payments. Some providers serving the nonprofit sector, like B Generous, offer funding like this to nonprofits. Their stated mission is to provide nonprofits with access to immediate capital so nonprofits can focus on their mission at hand, and worry less about fundraising.[47]

Reinvestment of Acquisition Revenue: One of the most widely available techniques for reinvestment is making the case for snowballing acquisition investment through the acquisition itself. The way this typically works is an organization works with its board to develop a reinvestment policy for acquisition.

For example, if an organization knows that its average new recurring gift is $40, the long-term value of recurring donors is $1,400, but it costs $400 on average to acquire that donor, the organization can reinvest up to 100 percent of the first twelve months of giving into further donor acquisition.

By reinvesting those months of giving back into acquisition, charities can cashflow and scale their subscription giving donor file in a fraction of the time of a slow, traditionally funded effort.

I'm not a lawyer or financial advisor, but if you can agree on a reasonable approach with your board and finance team, I've seen organizations double and quadruple their fundraising programs in a few short years using these approaches.

TAKEAWAY: New and unique financial approaches will continue to evolve that will enable charities to leverage the subscription economy and subscription trends to grow funding for programming by tapping into payment methods, new ways of giving, corporate partnerships, and financial reinvestment models to increase impact.

Let's now look at how the experience of becoming and staying a sustainer will get better.

CHAPTER 34
Donor Experience

WITH 97 PERCENT of the value of subscription donors being realized after the first gift, a sustainer-first mindset will lead to a focus on enhancing and improving the donor experience. As charities become more sustainer first, the donor experience will improve in several ways.

In the future, the recurring giving donor journey will rival the best subscription experiences.

Prediction: One-Click Sign-Up Experiences Will Become Commonplace

While the processes for signing up to give on a recurring basis have improved over the years compared to the ease of experiences like Amazon's 1-Click checkout, they are still cumbersome.

How many steps and fields would you expect the average person to work through to become one of your most valuable donors? I did a quick informal review of one of the nonprofit sector's best

In the future, the recurring giving donor journey will rival the best subscription experiences.

donation form experiences and found there were *seventeen* different form fields and steps required to complete a recurring gift sign-up.

In the future, signing up for recurring giving will be vastly simplified.

Part of the streamlined process will require payment technology innovations and consumer-friendly privacy and security. Some of this innovation will come from technology companies, some from financial institutions, and still others from nonprofit organizations.

Prediction: Alternate Recurring Giving Frequencies Will Be Increasingly Popular

A trend that has been growing for some time is offering subscription gifts at intervals other than monthly, such as annual or quarterly.

Historically, sustainer giving has been predominantly a monthly concept. But just like in the subscription world, some subscriptions make more sense as an annual payment. Similarly, organizations have seen success in offering quarterly and annual payment options.

Not every donor will want to give as often as monthly.

Alternative giving frequencies may help charities that have more significant upfront churn. For example, with face-to-face fundraising, there is often a period of heightened churn in the first two or three months. If the charity offers a quarterly or even annual subscription giving option, they effectively lock in 100 percent of the gift for that initial period, reducing churn.

In addition, we are starting to see higher frequencies than monthly. In the 2024 presidential election, entering the race relatively late in the game, Kamala Harris promoted a ten-dollar weekly recurring ask. Her campaign broke fundraising records in the opening weeks, including significant numbers of donors giving weekly.

There is a reason I've refrained from using the term "monthly giving" in this book. Recurring subscription giving does not necessarily have to occur monthly.

Prediction: Identity and Belonging Will Play an Increasingly Important Role in Subscription Giving

One thing we have seen throughout the history of philanthropy is that donors often give to express their values. Giving signals what the donor values—to themselves and others. This is most prominently displayed in giving to the arts, education, or healthcare, but every sector of philanthropy is impacted.

At the same time, identity is a topic of great importance in our modern culture. Who am I? What do I stand for? Who are we together? Identity goes beyond race, ethnicity, and gender. Identity is seen in the brands we wear, the cars we drive, and the flags we wave—metaphorical or physical.

I commonly hear charities find it a challenge to get donors to engage in community. That being said, I believe that *participation* in a charity-led community is not the same as *belonging* to that community. Donors may not participate in a charity-led community, but that does not mean that a sense of community, belonging, and connection with your cause does not contribute to their involvement with your cause.

Recurring subscription giving does not necessarily have to occur monthly.

More research and testing are needed in this area, but my hypothesis is that the value of belonging to a community of other individuals who believe passionately about a cause will increasingly influence the decisions that donors make to give to charities.

Identity, for some, is a way of saying to the world, "I belong. I care about this cause and feel like I'm a part of a greater whole." As Seth Godin says, "People like us do things like this."

Prediction: The Role of Influencers Will Evolve and Grow

Influencers have always played a role in promoting products and services through word of mouth, celebrity endorsements, testimonials, and so on. Over the years, charities have tapped into influencers to promote their cause, whether that includes actors for St. Jude Children's Research Hospital or musicians for Compassion International. Leveraging the celebrity and credibility of artists, musicians, athletes, and actors to promote a cause is not new, but the nature of influence is changing.

Today, the definition of an influencer has expanded. Influencers are no longer isolated to just "famous people." Anyone with an audience is a potential influencer—thought leaders, pastors, gamers, chefs, advocates, citizen journalists, and so on.

In addition, platforms like YouTube, TikTok, LinkedIn, X, and others have given individuals influence that was not possible in the previous generation.

This new form of influencer marketing is still developing, even on the consumer side. Platforms like Cameo are making the connection between influencers and organizations more accessible than ever before. Cameo promises to help you "Find the right celeb for any occasion."[48] They have thousands of influencers, from NFL legend Bo Jackson, Kevin O'Leary of *Shark Tank* fame, and Jesse Palmer, host of *The*

Bachelor. But they also have comedians, YouTubers, streamers, podcasters, and artists. For $250 to $10,000, these influencers will make a piece of content for your birthday party or fundraising campaign.

Who knows if these platforms will dominate in the years ahead, but the idea that a person of influence can partner with a nonprofit or brand is increasingly common. I see opportunities to expand upon the historical practice of partnering with musicians and celebrities to drive cause awareness and donations.

Prediction: Donors Will Churn More, Driven by Subscription Behavior

Recurring giving has proven to be different from subscriptions in one way—recurring giving programs have enjoyed far less churn than the typical consumer subscription.

On the surface, this makes sense. If I haven't used Netflix in a few months, I will cancel or pause my Netflix subscription. I'm not "giving" to Netflix in some charitable capacity—I'm paying for a product—one that needs to provide ongoing value. And if I'm not receiving that ongoing value, it's an easy decision to cancel.

We live in a world where consumers have no hesitation in canceling and restarting subscriptions. As consumers use applications like Rocket Money to track and manage all of their subscriptions, including monthly giving, it is foreseeable that donors will more readily cancel recurring giving.

It is reasonable to expect that as donors' expectations increase, we could see more volatility in recurring

> It is reasonable to expect that as donors' expectations increase, we could see more volatility in recurring giving in the future.

giving in the future. Charities must continue to invest in and improve their subscription giving programs to keep churn low.

TAKEAWAY: As recurring subscription giving programs continue to mature, the experience of becoming and staying a sustainer will improve, leading to easier, more delightful experiences, donor control, and choice, and an increased sense of community and belonging. The role of influencers will expand and evolve, and donors will be increasingly discerning about what they subscribe to, including their recurring charitable giving.

Let's conclude our journey by looking at sustainable giving's role in shaping philanthropy for the next generation and in addressing philanthropy's most pressing issue—the generosity crisis.

CHAPTER 35

The Generosity Crisis and the Role of Sustainable Giving

IN 2022, AUTHORS Nathan Chappell, Brian Crimmins, and Michael Ashley wrote a book called *The Generosity Crisis*.[49] Several people recommended the book to me over the next year and finally, in the summer of 2023, I started it. Several chapters in, I was blown away, fired up—and discouraged.

Many of the headlines about philanthropy over the past few decades have been about growth in overall giving. But those headlines mask an underlying dark truth—that while the total giving from individuals has been increasing, the total number of donors giving has been declining. For years, philanthropy has increasingly become concentrated among fewer, larger donors.

It was a wake-up call for an ongoing issue in philanthropy that I was vaguely familiar with, but Chappell and his coauthors piercingly illuminated—the number of Americans making charitable gifts has reached an all-time low. They go on to make the case that statistics indicate the percentages of people giving to charity annually could decline into the single digits in fewer than fifty years.

Generosity in America has been declining.

The book offers suggestions to address the generosity crisis, making a case for radical connection leveraging technology and personalization as part of the solution.

Generosity in America has been declining.

TAKEAWAY: Generosity in America is declining—fewer Americans are giving to charity than at any other time in history. The generosity crisis is a call to action. If you care about generosity in America, we've got a massive problem.

The question is, what are we going to do about the generosity crisis? What are you going to do? What can we do?

The Role of Sustainable Giving in the Generosity Crisis

Right around the time I was reading the book, I had the opportunity to interview Nathan on a podcast I cohost called *The Purpose & Profit Podcast*.

The question is, what are we going to do about the generosity crisis? What are you going to do?

After that interview, I couldn't help but reflect on the potential for sustainer giving in the subscription economy as one tool in our belt as charity leaders and compassionate donors to address the generosity crisis.

Amidst a torrent of discouraging headlines over the past couple of years, recurring sustainer giving has been the consistent bright spot, countering the decline in single-gift donors, lower retention, higher churn, and higher acquisition and cultivation costs.

Sustainable subscription giving is one of the most significant opportunities for charity leaders and those passionate about addressing the generosity crisis.

You and I have a role to play in addressing the generosity crisis.

We've been given an opportunity.

You and I can do something.

You can create a thriving community of supporters passionate about the cause.

You can create a resilient, sustainable income stream to empower us to do what we've been called.

What are you waiting for?

You and I have a role to play in addressing the generosity crisis.

The Rise of Sustainable Giving

How The Subscription Economy Is Transforming Recurring Giving And What Nonprofits Can Do To Benefit

Dave Raley

ADDENDUM: ACQUISITION AND CONVERSION CHANNELS

FOLLOWING ARE A list with brief descriptions of seventeen different channels often utilized in acquiring new recurring donors or recruiting existing. As you consider each, I highly recommend using the impact-effort matrix we discussed in chapter 18. It's a great tool to filter through and prioritize efforts.

- Events (A,C)
- Website (A,C)
- Artists (A)
- Video/TV (A,C)
- Face-to-Face (A)
- Direct Mail (C)
- Phone (C)
- Email (C)
- Social Media (A,C)
- Digital Media (A,C)
- Content/Earned Media (A,C)
- Search (A,C)
- Peer-to-Peer (A)
- Text/Mobile (C)
- Receipt Inserts (C)
- Collateral (A,C)
- Corporate/Church Relations (A)

Let's start with events, which can be useful for both acquiring new sustainers and converting existing ones.

Events (Acquisition and Conversion)

Events can take on a wide variety of formats and appearances. Some events are live and in-person, while others are virtual. Any gathering of individuals related to your cause is an event, whether that be a hosted dinner, a house party, a banquet or a gala, a 5K or another peer-to-peer event, volunteer rallies, seminars or workshops, townhall meetings, or even a telefundraising special.

The common denominator for events is a captive audience gathered for a reason, either an event unrelated to your cause, such as a concert or religious gathering, or an event specifically focused on your cause.

Website (Acquisition and Conversion)

Your website is the most important asset for acquiring and converting donors to recurring donors because it attracts people who are aware of you. Website visitors are ideal prospects for sustainer recruitment because they've elected to visit your website for some reason, meaning they have some level of awareness or interest in what you're doing.

There are a couple of critical areas of your website to consider—your home page and internal calls to action within a website on the most popular pages. In most cases on these interior pages, having a simple form or call out or call to action in the sidebar is good, but even better would be a direct call to action related to the content on the page. The next area to look at on your website are your donation pages. Each donation page, whether a landing page rich with content or a simple donation form, represents an opportunity to encourage donors to choose regular recurring giving. Further, consider the types of calls to action you can include during and just after the donation process.

Artists (Mostly Acquisition)

Artists and influencers can be a significant channel for sustainer acquisition. The right musician or influencer can become a personal advocate for your cause in addition to promoting your program at events such as concerts, conferences, and churches—anywhere they command the attention of people who are gathering. These influencers might be musicians, entertainers, pastors, celebrities, or social media personalities—anybody with an audience.

Video/Television (Acquisition and Conversion)

Video is a potent storytelling tool. It's visual and audio, and capturing viewers' attention is a great way to tell compelling stories and make a case for why the viewer should care and motivate them to take action.

There are several different forms of video, including DRTV (Direct Response Television), CTV (Connected Television), and streaming video. DRTV is "Any television advertising that asks consumers to respond directly to the company—usually either by calling a toll-free telephone number, sending an SMS message, or visiting a web site."[50] Connected Television (CTV) is similar to DRTV but "Refers to the practice of delivering ads through internet-connected television sets, where viewers stream digital content through apps, either built in or via devices like Roku, Apple TV, or gaming consoles."[51] Streaming video includes over the top (OTT) being streamed over the top of the internet, including streaming services such as Netflix, Disney+, Amazon Prime, and Hulu, and social media platforms such as YouTube, Twitch, and the like.

Video acquisition and conversion formats vary from long-form telethons to thirty-to-sixty-second CTV paid video spots to social media videos, including short- and long-form documentaries.

Face-to-Face (Mostly Acquisition)

Face-to-face fundraising involves a professional fundraiser approaching a member of the public to seek their financial support for a cause. According to the Professional Face-to-Face Fundraising Association, this type of fundraising could be in any public space—high-traffic public areas such as parks or high streets, retail stores, door-to-door, large entertainment events, or airports.[52] Also known as canvassing, face-to-face fundraising can provide tremendous scale for the right charity with the right offer and budget.

Face-to-face is much more common in Europe, but the PFFA estimates that more than 250,000 people in the United States commit to an ongoing or recurring donation through face-to-face fundraising each year. Some trade-offs to face-to-face involve a significant minimum budget to start, larger average gifts, and higher initial churn.

Direct Mail (Mostly Conversion)

Direct mail is the foundation of many single-gift fundraising programs, but it has an inconsistent track record when it comes to acquiring and converting donors to recurring giving.

Where it does work, direct mail is best used in the conversion of existing donors to recurring giving, particularly in new-donor onboarding programs.

Phone (Mostly Conversion)

While rarely used in acquisition, the phone has proven to be a highly effective channel for inviting existing single-gift donors to recurring giving, upgrading donors, and reactivating them.

Organizations that regularly utilize phone-based efforts will typically do one or a few concentrated campaigns focused on inviting existing one-time or lapsed monthly donors to give on a recurring basis. They often utilize modeling to identify the most likely donors to call first. Phone-based efforts also often include existing recurring donors, who are invited to increase their recurring gift amount or give a single additional gift for a specific need.

Email (Mostly Conversion)

Nothing beats email for the ability to directly and instantly reach out to individuals on an ongoing basis. In acquisition, email is either used to convert names or to acquire names and donors, but more often than not, email is used as a conversion channel to cultivate, promote, and convert donors to subscription giving.

Social Media (Acquisition and Conversion)

Social Media refers to any form of content, community, or promotion on social media platforms like Facebook, Instagram, Pinterest, TikTok, and so on. Social media for sustainer program growth falls into two types—paid and organic. Most successful sustainer program growth is due to paid social media promotion.

Paid social media can look like ads, or it can look like content. Social media also enables targeting of individuals using the power of artificial intelligence to identify the most likely to respond to a cause, using what is known as *lookalike audiences*. Lookalike modeling offers the ability to upload a list of your best individuals and target ads to people who "look like" those individuals.

Outside of lookalike modeling, other types of targeting include promoting content to your existing followers or subscribers and interest-based targeting. In interest-based targeting, you can target individuals who are interested in particular causes or topics that might be relevant to your cause.

Digital Media (Acquisition and Conversion)

Digital media is a cousin of social media and includes display ads, video ads, and content-oriented ads outside social media. Display advertising includes traditional paid banner ads and more unique advertising types like native advertising. Native ads look like content; you typically see them at the bottom of news articles, positioned as content with links. Display advertising can also include unique ads like pop-ups or push-downs on websites. The common denominator is paying to put a visually oriented advertisement in front of an individual.

Video ads are similar to display, but instead of static or lightly animated graphics, video ads use the power of video to catch a user's attention or to fit into a platform that is more video-oriented to reach users. Finally, we have content that can be paid for placement, such as a sponsored article, blog post, story, or other story.

Content/Earned Media (Acquisition and Conversion)

While paid advertising is typically the most immediate and directly impactful form of digital media marketing today, content and earned media can drive significant interest and traffic.

Earned media is when content is featured by another party without payment because it's relevant to that outlet's audience. Guest blog posts, podcast interviews, articles, written interviews, videos, and so on are examples of earned media. Each of these pieces of content can become powerful online "outposts" that drive interest and traffic.

Search—Organic and Paid (Acquisition and Conversion)

Organic search refers to the natural ranking of the pages on your site based on specific terms, while paid search offers more control as you can bid on specific terms and direct the user to particular landing pages and content in a paid ad, whereas an organic ad is not changeable.

Charities tend to leverage paid search primarily to direct traffic to pages and content related to recurring giving, due to the control that paid search affords, versus being left to the whims of search engines when it comes to organic search.

Peer-to-Peer (Mostly Acquisition)

Peer-to-peer, or P2P, involves asking existing donors to invite other donors to join with them. It is often associated with single gifts

("Sponsor me for the 5k!"), but can and does result in acquiring new recurring donors.

For example, charity: water famously allows people to donate on their birthday to encourage people to give to the organization. Another example is Compassion International's Compassion Sunday, where each year Compassion Child sponsors are invited to host a Compassion Sunday, which involves sharing about the program at a local church gathering. In this way, recurring donor sponsors are helping to get more sponsors.

Text/Mobile (Mostly Conversion)

Text and mobile messaging are currently the most intimate, direct form of communication with donors. Increasing numbers of nonprofits are using this to connect with their audiences.

Text messaging is associated with higher engagement, higher open rates, and more intimacy. It enables you to help donors to feel more like insiders. It's less crowded as a communication space than email or social media and more immediate and intimate. This means it's one to handle with extreme care. You don't want to be known as the organization that spams your people. I don't recommend text messaging if you only want to use it for fundraising or recurring donor recruitment because you can quickly burn out your list.

The charities that are using text messaging well are doing so as a communications tool to benefit donors—to keep them up to date with timely or inspirational content or to inspire and benefit them. In those cases, charities have the ability to periodically message donors with fundraising asks.

Receipt Inserts (Conversion)

Receipts are focused on affirming the donor and, along the way can be a great place to communicate about recurring giving. This includes both email and mailed receipts. Often, the strategy is to tell a story of how their gift has made a difference, affirm the donor, and then include an insert of a secondary call to action to promote recurring giving.

Collateral (Acquisition and Conversion)

Collateral refers to any assets used to describe or promote one's subscription giving program. Typically used more passively, collateral includes promotional inserts and distribution in various locations.

There are other places where sustainer program promotions can be inserted alongside other communications, including newspapers, bill stuffers, magazines, newsletters, and books. Beyond inserts, there are physical locations where charities can contact donors and potential donors. These include retail stores, places of worship, coffee shops, restaurants, or places of business.

Anywhere you have a likely good fit audience and a partner who is willing to distribute or set out collateral is worth considering.

Corporate/Church Relations (Mostly Acquisition)

Institutions like corporations and places of worship can be significant sources of names and new recurring donors. They can be challenging opportunities to pursue, but they can be excellent drivers of program growth with the right program and relationships.

Typically, the charities that see success with corporate or church relations have another good reason to be engaged—they are involved with the company's employee giving program, for instance, or speak regularly in places of worship.

NOTES

1 Giving USA 2023 Annual Report, https://givingusa.org/.
2 *Recurring Giving Report 2024*, Neon One. https://neonone.com/resources/recurring-giving-report/.
3 *Giving USA 2024 Annual Report*, Giving USA Foundation. https://givingusa.org/
4 M+R, *M+R Benchmarks Report 2024*, https://mrbenchmarks.com/
5 Tobias Jung, Susan D. Phillips, and Jenny Harrow, eds., *The Routledge Companion to Philanthropy* (Milton Park, Oxfordshire, UK: Routledge, 2016).
6 Wesley Lindahl, *Principles of Fundraising. Theory and Practice* (Burlington, MA: Jones & Bartlett Learning, 2010).
7 Hillary Kaell, “The Long History of Child Sponsorship, c. 1700–1950,” *Historical Research* 95, no. 267 (November 2021): 45–61.
8 Jung, Phillips, and Harrow, eds., *The Routledge Companion to Philanthropy.*
9 Wikipedia, s.v. “*Reader’s Digest*,” https://en.wikipedia.org/wiki/Reader%27s_Digest
10 S. L. C. Clapp, “The Beginnings of Subscription Publication in the Seventeenth Century,” *Modern Philology* (1931), https://doi.org/10.1086/387957

11 Subscription Trade Association, "Subscription Commerce Industry Outlook," SUBTA, accessed August 20, 2024, https://subta.com/annual-report-2023/.

12 Zuora, "The SEI Report: Recurring Growth Strategies for Total Monetization," Zuora, April 2024, https://www.zuora.com/resources/subscription-economy-index/.

13 Daniela Coppola, "Subscription Economy: Global Market Size 2025," Statista, 2022, https://www.statista.com/statistics/1295064/market-size-digital-subscription-economy-worldwide-by-segment/.

14 Giving USA 2023 Report, https://givingusa.org/.

15 Lovemoney Staff, "The Cost of the World's Biggest Problems, and Who Could Afford to Fix Them," loveMONEY, December 15, 2021, https://www.lovemoney.com/galleries/68916/the-cost-of-the-worlds-biggest-problems-and-who-could-afford-to-fix-them; Rob Moore, "What Would It Cost to End Homelessness in America?" Scioto Analysis, January 16, 2024, https://www.sciotoanalysis.com/news/2024/1/16/what-would-it-cost-to-end-homelessness-in-america.

16 Fundraising Effectiveness Project, "Year-End Challenges in Q4 2023 as Fundraising Metrics Decline | Association of Fundraising Professionals," AFP Global, 2024, https://afpglobal.org/news/year-end-challenges-q4-2023-fundraising-metrics-decline.

17 Robbie K. Baxter, *The Membership Economy: Find Your Super Users, Master the Forever Transaction, and Build Recurring Revenue* (New York: McGraw-Hill Education, 2015).

18 Tien Tzuo and Gabe Weisert, *Subscribed: Why the Subscription Model Will Be Your Company's Future—and What to Do About It* (New York: Penguin Publishing Group, 2018).

19 Robbie K. Baxter, *The Forever Transaction: How to Build a Subscription Model So Compelling, Your Customers Will Never Want to Leave* (New York: McGraw-Hill Education. 2020).

20 M+R, *M+R Benchmarks Report 2024*, https://mrbenchmarks.com/.

21 Neon One, *Recurring Giving Report 2024*, https://neonone.com/resources/recurring-giving-report/.

22 Dataro, *Dataro Fundraising Benchmark Report 2023*, https://landing.dataro.io/2023-benchmark-report-usa.

23 Classy, "The State of Modern Philanthropy 2022 | The Path to Lasting Donor Connections," https://donationtrends.classy.org/.

24 Blackbaud, *Blackbaud Luminate Online Benchmark Report 2022*, https://www.blackbaud.com/industry-insights/resources/nonprofit-organizations/blackbaud-luminate-online-benchmark-report-2022.

25 Blackbaud, *Blackbaud donorCentrics Sustainer Summit Benchmarking*, https://adirectsolution.com/wp-content/uploads/2024/04/BB_FY2023_SustainersummitWebinar.pdf.

26 ECFA, *ECFA 2023 State of Giving*, https://www.ecfa.org/stateofgiving/.

27 NextAfter, *The Nonprofit Recurring Giving Benchmark Study*, https://www.recurringgiving.com/.

28 Steven Screen, "What Is a Fundraising 'Offer'?—Better Fundraising Co." Better Fundraising, 2018, https://betterfundraising.com/what-is-a-fundraising-offer-infographic/.

29 Wikipedia, s.v. "marketing mix," https://en.wikipedia.org/wiki/Marketing_mix.

30 Alexandra Twin, "The 4 Ps of Marketing: What They Are & How to Use Them Successfully," Investopedia, https://www.investopedia.com/terms/f/four-ps.asp.

31 Twin, "The 4 Ps of Marketing."

32 Twin, "The 4 Ps of Marketing."

33 Twin, "The 4 Ps of Marketing."

34 Dan Pallotta, *Uncharitable: How Restraints on Nonprofits Undermine Their Potential* (Waltham, MA: Brandeis University Press, 2022).

35 Lark Editor Team. "Impact Effort Matrix: A Powerful Tool for Productivity," Lark, 2023, https://www.larksuite.com/en_us/topics/productivity-glossary/impact-effort-matrix.

36 Nathan Hill, "How to Write Your Nonprofit Value Proposition," NextAfter. https://www.nextafter.com/blog/how-to-write-your-nonprofit-value-proposition/.

37 NextAfter, "The Ultimate A/B Testing Guide for Online Fundraising," https://www.nextafter.com/ab-testing-guide/.

38 Elizabeth Hopper and Cynthia Vinney, "Maslow's Hierarchy of Needs Explained—Psychology," ThoughtCo, 2024, https://www.thoughtco.com/maslows-hierarchy-of-needs-4582571.

39 Zerocap, "What is Price Anchoring?" 2023, https://zerocap.com/insights/snippets/what-is-price-anchoring/.

40 Zapier, "Zapier: Automate Your Work Today," https://zapier.com/.

41 Claire Axelrad, "Should We Ask Donors to Cover Donation Processing Fees?" Bloomerang, https://bloomerang.co/blog/ask-an-expert-should-we-ask-donors-to-cover-donation-processing-fees/.

42 Erica Waasdorp, "How Small Recurring Gifts Lead to the Ultimate Gift," Bloomerang, https://bloomerang.co/blog/how-small-recurring-gifts-lead-to-the-ultimate-gift.

43 Wikipedia, s.v. "Digital Wallet," https://en.wikipedia.org/wiki/Digital_wallet.

44 David Morris, "Payments Trends to Watch in 2024," eMarketer, 2024. https://content-na1.emarketer.com/payments-trends-watch-2024#page-charts.

45 National Philanthropic Trust, *Donor-Advised Fund Report: Grants to Charities Increase 9%, Hitting a New Record High*, NonProfit PRO, 2023, https://www.nonprofitpro.com/article/donor-advised-fund-report-grants-charities-increase-9/.

46 Katherine Rea, "We Donated $25,000 to Foster Kids!" KiwiCo, https://www.kiwico.com/blog/kiwico-news/we-donated-25000-to-foster-kids.

47 “The Nation’s Leading Nonprofit Lender,” B Generous, https://bgenerous.com/.

48 “About Us,” Cameo, https://www.cameo.com/about.

49 Brian Crimmins, Nathan Chappell, and Michael Ashley, *The Generosity Crisis: The Case for Radical Connection to Solve Humanity’s Greatest Challenges* (Hoboken, NJ: Wiley, 2022).

50 Wikipedia, s.v. “Direct response television,” https://en.wikipedia.org/wiki/Direct_response_television.

51 Melissa Yap and Frankie Karrer. n.d. “What Is Connected TV? How CTV Advertising Works (2024).” MNTN. https://mountain.com/blog/connected-tv-advertising/.

52 Professional Face-to-Face Fundraising Association, https://pf-faus.org/.

ACKNOWLEDGMENTS

IT TAKES A village to put ideas into the world, especially if you want anyone to read them. I'd like to thank many of the people who have been instrumental for the past couple of years in making this book.

First, to my wife, Heather, and our daughters, Paige and Emma. You've been a tremendous source of support and encouragement throughout this process. Paige, I love your discernment—you are always willing to provide input and creative ideas. Emma, I love your caring empathetic spirit and enthusiasm to help in any way you can. Heather, you are wise. You believe in me. You fight for me. You listen to me. You ask good questions. I love you.

To my collaborators and sounding boards along the way—there are too many of you to name, but I'll try a few—Brad O'Brien, Dana Snyder, Dusty Rhodes, Erik Tomalis, Gabe Cooper, Jessica Lalley, Teresa Weaver, Tom Dean, Tom Harrison.

To Erica Waasdorp—you literally wrote the book on monthly giving—*two* actually! To have your encouragement, your wisdom, and your direct feedback on the concepts and words throughout this book have made it indelibly better. Thank you.

To Abigail Morse and Grace Martinson—you have been a tremendous support over the past year. Your diligence, attention to detail, and tenacity have been a huge blessing.

To my publishing and editorial team at Streamline Books—Donnel McLohon, thank you for keeping the project moving and for helping this first-time author understand the process. Gin Smith and Kiska Carr, for poring over my words and taking them to another level of consistency and polish. Nathaniel Roy and Alice Briggs, for your thoughtful and sharp eye for cover design and interior layout. And to Alex Demczak and Will Severns for pulling together a quality team of craftspeople.

To thoughts that contributed through interviews and insights—Allen Thornburgh, Amy Konary, Bobb Biehl, Brady Josephson, Jon Van Wyk, Mark Becker, Nathan Chappell, Nathan Hill, Peter Greer, Robbie Kellman Baxter, Steve Woodworth, and Tim Kachuriak. Your experiences and wisdom will help shape the future of our world, and I'm grateful for you.

To the clients I've been blessed to serve—thank you. When I founded Imago Consulting, I wondered if I could invest half of my time in learning, researching, and uncovering insights and the other half of my time working with leaders and organizations to strategically apply those insights. So far, so good! You are a joy to work with, and I've loved seeing your growth, personally and organizationally.

ABOUT THE AUTHOR

Dave Raley
Founder, Imago Consulting
Cohost, *Purpose & Profit* Podcast
Author, *The Rise of Sustainable Giving* and The Wave Report
National Keynote Speaker

Dave Raley has worked with or trained hundreds of nonprofits over the past two decades, ranging from small charities to multibillion-dollar organizations. He's the author of *The Wave Report*—a weekly column on trends and lessons leaders can learn to apply to grow themselves and their organizations.

Dave speaks, writes, and consults on the topics of fundraising, marketing, innovation, and recurring revenue. His written work has been published in *Outcomes* Magazine, *DMAW Marketing AdVents*, and *Instigate* Magazine.

Dave has toured the nation giving keynotes, seminars, and workshops on topics such as "Sustainable Giving in the Subscription Economy," "Where Innovation Goes Wrong," "The Myths of Innovation," and "How AI is Transforming Marketing and Fundraising."

Dave led as executive vice president of one of the nation's largest agencies specializing in marketing and fundraising for faith-based organizations—Masterworks. Dave also serves as a board member and advisor to several nonprofits.

Dave founded Imago Consulting, a firm that helps nonprofits and businesses create profitable growth through sustainable innovation.

Dave is cofounder of *The Purpose & Profit Podcast*, a show dedicated to uncovering the surprising ideas at the intersection of causes and brands. The show has featured prominent leaders from the for-profit and nonprofit sector, including guests from nonprofits such as charity: water, International Justice Mission, Compassion International, and brands such as Disney, Chick-fil-A, Oreo, and Pizza Hut.

Book Dave to Speak

If you would like to explore having Dave speak at your next event, visit:

Book Dave to Speak at
www.imago.consulting/speaking

FREE RESOURCES

Receive Your Free Sustainable Giving Assessment

After years of research and hundreds of hours, we've developed a sustainable giving growth self-assessment for nonprofit leaders and fundraisers. This free assessment includes twenty questions and takes just ten minutes to complete.

Your personalized results will be a helpful guide as you seek to grow recurring subscription giving.

Take the Free Sustainable Giving Assessment at
www.imago.consulting/assessment

Get Free Weekly Insights with The Wave Report

Every Friday, Dave sends out The Wave Report, highlighting trends and insights in innovation, fundraising, marketing, technology, and of course, subscriptions and subscription giving.

Sign Up for Free Weekly Insights and Trends at
www.imago.consulting/wavereport

www.ingramcontent.com/pod-product-compliance
Lightning Source LLC
Chambersburg PA
CBHW071539210326
41597CB00019B/3056

* 9 7 9 8 8 9 1 6 5 2 1 0 1 *